PRAISE FOR
INTENTIONAL

This book, *Intentional*, is based on God's Word, and God always asks us to do things that work for real, regular people. Your life will become more intentional if you read and implement the practices in this book. Brandon Guindon is a disciple-making practitioner, not a theorist. Brandon and his wife, Amber, have personally discipled people for many years now. Brandon knows, without having to think about it, how to be intentional. Brandon began his ministry career on staff at Real Life Ministries, and his intentionality helped to increase our number of small groups exponentially. He helped develop training that has spanned the globe. He went on to plant a discipleship-based church that has grown and thrived. He raises up people from within to disciple others, to serve on staff, and to plant churches nationally and internationally. If you want to become more intentional in your life, this book should be your next read.

—Jim Putman, author and senior
pastor of Real Life Ministries

Intentional is an extraordinary book that powerfully captures how to do the work of disciple making. Author Brandon Guindon does not give us a book of theory but a personal example of a multiplier and how he intentionally lives that out. In an era where church leaders are looking for resources to guide them in how to return to disciple making, *Intentional* should be at the top of your list!

—Dave Ferguson, author, president and
cofounder of Exponential, lead pastor of
Community Christian Church

I have known Brandon Guindon for twenty years and paid witness to the lived-out principles that he puts forward. Brandon holds up a mirror to help show us who Jesus intends us to be. Take the *Intentional* journey, and you will be better for it. This book will challenge and encourage you, and in the cooperation with the Holy Spirit you will be changed by it.

—**Mark "Moose" Bright,** director of the
Relational Discipleship Network

Brandon Guindon shows us the practical elements of disciple making. For higher education to thrive today, we must help students equip local everyday disciples to trust and follow Jesus. I recommend his book *Intentional* to help us do this better.

—**Tony Twist,** president and CEO of
TCM International Institute

I am grateful for how Brandon passionately explores disciple making in his book *Intentional*. Obviously, we need a return to disciple making in this generation. As you work through each page of inspiring story and practical guidance, you be refreshed by God's calling for the church to make disciples and see church multiplication accelerate through your ministry.

—**Jason Stewart,** executive director
of mobilization at Exponential

Intentional is the only book on discipleship that I am aware of that not only gives you biblically founded principles but also has the personal stories and illustrations to help the reader get a picture of what discipleship really looks like. The book makes a case for being an intentional disciple maker and what that looks like on a day-to-day basis. This explanation includes personal stories from other disciple makers as well as penetrating self-assessment. This book is what I needed to read to help me in growing as a disciple who helps make disciples!

—**Matt Dabbs,** church planter at Backyard Church

Brandon knows how to tell a story and speak to others in a way that just keeps you reading or listening. The reason the stories are so good is that they are based on something much more profound, the reality of Brandon's life and work on those around him. This is practical, yes, but it is more powerful than anything else. *Intentional* is a special testimony of God's work through a pastor and of his family.

—**Bill Hull,** author of *No Longer a Bystander* and *I Will Not Bow Down*

Intentional simplifies the often-overwhelming subject of discipleship. Brandon Guindon artfully leads you through the practical process of unleashing your inner disciple maker! In reading *Intentional*, you'll discover that making disciples is more natural than you think. This is an enjoyable read and a must-have for every Christian. Frankly, the principles in this book apply to training leaders in business and any other arena that benefits from mentoring as well.

—**Wes Beavis,** PsyD, clinical psychologist, author of *Let's Talk About Ministry Burnout*

Brandon Guidon has knocked it out of the park with this great book! Making disciples in today's world is not easy, and Brandon puts it all into perspective by sharing how to apply the eight practices of disciple making. We have a disciplined road map with *Intentional*. But ultimately, discipleship takes people who are trained and have the heart and desire to win people for Christ. So let's go make disciples as Jesus commands in Matthew 28:19–20 and how Brandon describes in this great book.

—**Douglas J. Crozier,** president and chief
executive officer, the Solomon Foundation

Practical is the word I would use to describe Brandon Guindon's book *Intentional*. In a sea of books that offer theory, Guindon provides practical help with everyday discipleship, using snapshots from his own life and experience. It's a great guide for anyone looking for help with a hands-on approach. I highly recommend it!

—**Jerry Harris,** publisher of Christian Standard
Media, teaching pastor at The Crossing

INTENTIONAL

INTENTIONAL

Living Out the Eight Principles
of Disciple Making

BRANDON GUINDON

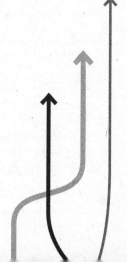

ZONDERVAN REFLECTIVE

Intentional
Copyright © 2023 by Brandon M. Guindon

Requests for information should be addressed to:
Zondervan, *3900 Sparks Dr. SE, Grand Rapids, Michigan 49546*

Zondervan titles may be purchased in bulk for educational, business, fundraising, or sales promotional use. For information, please email SpecialMarkets@Zondervan.com.

ISBN 978-0-310-15522-5 (audio)

Library of Congress Cataloging-in-Publication Data

Names: Guindon, Brandon M., 1974- author.
Title: Intentional : living out the eight principles of disciple making / Brandon Guindon.
Description: Grand Rapids : Zondervan, 2023.
Identifiers: LCCN 2023002354 (print) | LCCN 2023002355 (ebook) | ISBN 9780310155201 (paperback) | ISBN 9780310155218 (ebook)
Subjects: LCSH: Discipling (Christianity) | Evangelistic work. | Christian life. | BISAC: RELIGION / Christian Ministry / Discipleship | RELIGION / Christian Living / Leadership & Mentoring
Classification: LCC BV4520 .G85 2023 (print) | LCC BV4520 (ebook) | DDC 253--dc23/eng/20230420
LC record available at https://lccn.loc.gov/2023002354
LC ebook record available at https://lccn.loc.gov/2023002355

Cover design and art: Emily Weigel
Interior design: Kait Lamphere

Printed in the United States of America

23 24 25 26 27 28 29 30 31 32 /TRM/ 13 12 11 10 9 8 7 6 5 4 3 2 1

This book is filled with stories from my life that exist because of those who intentionally invested in me throughout the years. Living an intentional life is learned. No one has taught me more about the intentional principles than these people.

———————

To Amber, my amazing wife. Your incredible intentionality with our kids has inspired me countless times. Your sacrifice for and investment in our kids truly exemplifies the development of potential. I am forever grateful for you and your support. Without it I would not be the man I am today.

———————

To Desalegn and Tigst. I dedicate this book to you and your relentless work for King Jesus. You have unconditionally loved me and the folks I have brought over the years to your amazing country of Ethiopia. Thank you for being examples of what it means to be interruptible and how to stand firm when living out the Great Commission becomes difficult.

———————

To my parents, Bugs and Donna Guindon. Your constant support and encouragement have allowed me to live out the calling God put in my life. Even when it was hard, you have been willing to speak truth into my life and release me to go and live out what God called me to do. Thank you.

CONTENTS

FOREWORD

The Greek word *mathēteuō* is a single word found in Jesus' final mandate to his disciples in Matthew 28:19–20. It's also the most important Greek word in that mandate. Jesus said: "Therefore go and *mathēteuō* of all nations, baptizing them in the name of the Father and of the Son and of the Holy Spirit, and teaching them to obey everything I have commanded you. And surely, I am with you always, to the very end of the age." In this passage, *mathēteuō* is in the imperative mode—the form of a command—and that one word typically translates into two English words: *make disciples.*

Greek dictionaries flesh out the meaning of this one word in several ways: "make disciples," "train in discipleship," "to disciple," "to instruct," "to make apprentices." But Jesus' mandate is simple enough—that we *make disciples.* Yes, we must go; yes, we must baptize; yes, we must teach obedience to his commands; and yes, we must remember Jesus' presence will be with us to the end. But these other expressions are all contingent phrases that explain key parts of that key imperative in the Greek text: *make disciples.*

Jesus said *we must make disciples*. This means we take people and, *by what we do*, people become disciples of Jesus or become better disciples of Jesus. He put the onus on us. Yes, he promised to be with us in the process, helping us (Matthew 28:20). Yes, he teaches elsewhere that the Holy Spirit is at work in our disciple making (2 Corinthians 3:2–3). Still . . . he said we are to do it. If we take this command seriously, many of us honestly respond with an important question.

How do I make disciples?

Let me suggest that one key word captures the posture we need to have in response to this command of Jesus: *intentional*.

Jesus gives us many things to do. But behind all we do is something else, something essential to being a disciple maker. You must be *intentional* in all that you do.

Intentional means it is "done on purpose"—deliberately. And in this new book in the discipleship.org series, Brandon Guindon shows us how to cultivate this essential posture of effective discipleship. It's not complicated if we adopt an intentional strategy and mindset.

For those who are nervous about reading a complicated book with lofty ideas that never make a practical difference, let me assure you right now, before you even start: *this is an easy-to-read book, written in a relaxed tone, filled with lots of stories.*

Brandon has written several books and has years of experience as a pastor and disciple maker, but I believe this is his signature book. It best expresses his personal life mission statement: "I must motivate and inspire people to master the art of relational discipleship." Brandon invites you into his heart, his mind, and his purpose in life and both motivates and inspires us to fulfill Jesus' final mandate through simple but profound points illustrated by stories of hunting, the tragic accident and near death of his daughters, and how he himself was discipled. Of course, he also shares practical suggestions rooted in how he has discipled others over the past two decades of life and ministry. As a bonus, he provides us with great questions at the end of each chapter to facilitate discussion with others.

Brandon is the real deal. He lives what he writes about everyday—as a church planter, lead pastor, father, husband, and national and international trainer of disciple-making churches. He is one of the most highly effective church leaders in the United States. The fruit of his life and disciple making is clear, profound, and far reaching.

I plan to ask everyone on the staff and in the eldership at the church I lead to read this book. It is joyful and easy to follow, yet it is also a profound journey that will help every one of us to effectively develop the strategy and mindset summed up in that one very important word.

Bobby Harrington, pastor,
author, and CEO of RENEW.org
and Discipleship.org

AN INTENTIONAL LIFE

I grew up in Alaska. By age twelve I had enough wild adventures that friends encouraged me to write a book. Shooting a moose, catching salmon on rivers, and flying in floatplanes were all part of a normal day. And central to all of these stories was my dad, Bugs Guindon.

My dad was a man born in the wrong century. You might describe him as a mountain man or pioneer. If he had lived in the 1800s, he would have been one of those crazy guys who, upon hearing of rumors of gold in California, would have struck out with minimal supplies and gone in search of adventure and treasure. My father took our family on countless adventures, some of which did involve searching for gold. He's the type who would have volunteered for the Lewis and Clark Expedition without hesitation. I'm proud to call this man of incredible abilities, intuitive nature, and fearlessness my father.

In addition to having an adventurous spirit, my dad is also a jack-of-all-trades. With a little duct tape and baling wire, he can repair almost anything, at least well enough to get a job done. He is naturally able to figure out solutions and solve problems, and although he is incredibly talented, he does everything with humility, assuming anyone else could do exactly what he does.

While I share my father's adventurous spirit, I lack some of his natural, intuitive abilities. God designed me to be curious. I'm always interested in understanding how things work and even more curious about people, how they think and function. God made me to be a person who wants to be effective and successful at whatever I am doing. My wife, Amber, teases that when we go on vacation, I vacation "type A." My rest often looks like an intense search for knowledge and understanding. Whether I'm in a museum or restaurant or on a tour of a historic site, I want to understand how things were done. How did the chef make that meal? How were those things built? Why did those people two hundred years ago do what they did? My curiosity can almost drive people crazy.

Growing up, I was inspired by all the things my dad could do. I longed to have his intuitive sense of how to get a job done or how to fix a certain problem. Yet I was constantly frustrated. My curiosity left me wanting to understand, but my dad rarely offered to explain what he did. He just did it. So I was often left to figure things out on my own. Sure, my dad was willing to help me if I asked him, but most of the time I was left alone to puzzle out a solution. My dad was rarely intentional in passing his knowledge along to others, including his son.

When I came to Christ, I pursued the Bible with that same curiosity. Much like I would follow the directions in a recipe to cook a meal or study war strategies to better understand how some ancient military unit won a battle, I wanted to understand what it meant to follow Christ. I wanted to know every detail, as much as I possibly could. I pursued understanding the life of Christ with fervor, trying to grasp what it would have been like to follow him. When I studied the life of Christ early in my walk, I began to see that Jesus was incredibly intentional in everything he did. He modeled through his actions every truth he taught.

GOD'S PROVISION

I knew I wanted to live a strong Christian life, but I lacked a model for what that looked like. My parents did not know the Lord, yet my upbringing had instilled in me a drive to ask questions and learn. God, in his loving-kindness, put several people in my life to teach me the importance of intentionality.

When Amber and I first began dating, I spent a tremendous amount of time with her parents, both strong Christian people who modeled a transparent walk with the Lord. My mother-in-law, Joan, shared with me her own struggles and successes in her Christian walk. I remember, even before Amber and I were married, having conversations in which I asked Joan countless questions, and she taught me what it meant to seek the Holy Spirit to guide me. She taught me about having an intentional devotional time and how to press into God through his Word. She modeled for me the foundational practices essential to growing a healthy relationship with Christ.

Earl, my father-in-law, was also very intentional in shaping my understanding of how to follow Christ. He and I went on hikes and spent time together at the shooting range. We shared common interests, and during that time, he asked me questions about my own walk with Jesus. He answered countless questions and provided a wealth of information. He taught me basic Christian evidences and biblical history. He modeled patience as he helped me connect the dots of how the Bible came to be and how it was written. Along with imparting a great deal of knowledge, he also modeled what it meant to be a husband and father. He was not perfect, but he was real. And I knew that both Joan and Earl were intentional in their commitment to follow Jesus Christ.

Two years after Amber and I married, God called me into vocational ministry. I took my first steps into this calling at Real Life Ministries in Post Falls, Idaho, when I was hired as their small groups pastor. I had no Bible college degree, just a strong desire to learn and a heart full of questions. God continued to provide men and women in my life who modeled not only good ministry but remarkable faith in Christ.

Jim Putman, lead pastor at Real Life Ministries, was both my boss and one of my closest friends. Jim showed me what it meant to be a shepherd, and for fourteen years I served alongside him and we shared thousands of car rides together. Whether on a hunting trip or visiting someone in the hospital, we traveled the roads of north Idaho together. Sometimes we discussed ministry or life, but often I would sit in the passenger seat listening to him as he talked with someone on the phone. I listened to Jim as he made thousands of phone calls. He would call people he hadn't seen at church or who he knew were sick or had lost a job. Jim cared. He called just to check on people and see how they were doing. And in doing this, he modeled for me what it looks like to shepherd people intentionally.

Jim Blazin was another mentor God provided in my life. Jim modeled for me what it looks like to have intentional hunger and discipline to study and know God's Word. Numerous times we sat together talking about the Bible. We processed how the Word of God guided our delivery of ministry. Jim also spoke a great deal into my life about how the Holy Spirit guides us. His friendship and partnership in ministry were an even greater inspiration to me. His eyes would light up every time he would share some biblical truth. We walked together for years, building and leading the small group ministry at Real Life, and God provided Jim not only as a mentor but as a friend in my life.

Shortly after I went into ministry, God sent a man named Dan Lynch to Real Life. Dan mentored me as he taught me the Word of God and how to study the Bible. Most importantly, Dan modeled a holistic, healthy walk with Jesus. He patiently explained to me the spiritual priorities I should have in my life as a pastor. He taught me the importance of fasting and having an attitude of prayer. Dan also modeled how all of these spiritual components functioned in a marriage. He demonstrated a healthy spiritual walk with Jesus and with his wife.

And finally, I must mention my dear friend Lydia Grubb. Jim (yes, another Jim) and Lydia Grubb were one of the founding couples who planted Real Life Ministries. Lydia worked on staff with me for all those years at Real Life, investing in my life and modeling what it means to walk in faith. She showed me what it means to be interruptible. She also demonstrated what it looks like to stand firm when things get hard. Regardless of what was happening in her own life, if I was struggling, she would stop what she was doing and we would pray together.

God always gave her words that encouraged me to stand firm in my faith.

All of these individuals—Joan, Earl, Jim Putman, Jim Blazin, Dan Lynch, and Lydia Grubb—had tremendous influence in my life. But that influence was not by accident. Each of them intentionally invested in me. Without them I would never be where I'm at today in ministry. And now, looking back, I can see how the people who invested in my life modeled for me what it means to be an *intentional* disciple maker.

I am grateful for their investment and for God's provision through these relationships. Each of these faithful servants was doing their part, and God certainly was doing his part. But I had to do my part too. Each of us has a role to play, and if we hope to grow in our own walk with the Lord and then become someone who disciples others, we must learn to be intentional. We must learn to take up the mantle and the mission that Jesus has given us. The King of the universe has issued an edict, a commissioning, that every single person who surrenders their life to him must now go out into the world and be his disciple. And we are called to make disciples as well, intentionally investing what God has given us and taught us in the lives of others, in word, deed, and prayer.

That's the focus of this book. I'm hoping to pass along what others have taught me, to do for you what many others have done for me. My hope is to motivate and inspire you to live a life that is intentionally focused on the great calling Jesus has for each of us. I want you to know exactly what your next steps will be as you go into the world to make disciples.

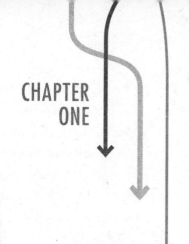

UNCONSCIOUS CAPABLE

On October 28, 2016, our family's lives were radically changed when our two daughters, Emma and Olivia, were in a car accident on their way to a softball tournament. A Ford F250 pickup truck T-boned their car, and both girls were severely injured. Olivia was flown by helicopter to the world-renowned Houston Medical Center. Sixteen skull fractures, a compound fractured jaw, a broken sternum, a brain bleed, and oxygen on the brain presented nearly impossible odds for Olivia to survive. Doctors gave her a 3 percent chance of survival. Even if she did survive, her likelihood of having any kind of functional life was slim. Our family faced what seemed to be an impossible mountain to climb.

Emma, our oldest, spent five days in the hospital, and for years following the accident, she suffered symptoms resulting from a severe concussion. Olivia, who was fourteen at the time, spent the next eighty-seven days in the hospital. For the first twenty-one days, she lay in a coma, on a ventilator. Ever so slowly, she began to respond as God healed her body, cell by cell. Eventually Olivia was transferred to a pediatric neuro rehabilitation center where she began the long, arduous journey of relearning almost everything. I learned more about traumatic brain injury and physical therapy than I ever cared to know. God was giving me nuggets of gold that I didn't recognize at the time. Those nuggets of truth would later impact my life and ministry.

As painful as that time was for our entire family, not only did God work a miracle in Olivia, but he also taught us about his miraculous power as we lived out his plan. We spent countless hours at Olivia's side as she relearned how to walk, talk, swallow, tie her shoes, and eat with silverware. We even joked at times that she had to relearn how to blink. The process was painful, but as God promised, he was working things out for his purposes. I never want to go through it again, but I'm grateful for the lessons we learned, and I'm grateful that I can pass the lessons on to those with whom God has allowed me to cross paths.

During Olivia's time in rehab, we learned a concept that I want to share with you, a principle that applies to intentional disciple making. Whenever the brain suffers a traumatic injury, many of the actions learned since infancy are lost. In Olivia's case, almost every physical movement had to be relearned. To help us in this process of relearning, the doctors and nurses taught us a principle called the Four Stages of Competence. They explained to us that Olivia would go through these stages as she completed her rehabilitation: unconscious incapable, conscious incapable, conscious capable, and unconscious capable.

Unconscious incapable: The individual does not understand or know how to do something. He or she is unaware of the skill and unable to perform it. Recognition of the deficit is nonexistent.

Conscious incapable: The individual has recognition and value of the new skill but is incapable of performing it. When beginning to attempt the new skill, mistakes become vital to learning.

Conscious capable: The individual understands and knows how to perform the task. However, demonstrating the skill or knowledge may necessitate breaking it down into steps and requires intense concentration.

Unconscious capable: The individual has had so much practice with a skill that it has become "second nature" and can be performed easily, even while executing another task. The individual may be able to teach it to others, depending on how and when it was learned.

When the car accident occurred, both girls were experienced, talented softball players who were being recruited to play college softball. Emma was an outstanding pitcher, and Olivia, a high school freshman, was known by many universities as one of the top catchers in the country. Both girls had spent countless hours throughout their young lives throwing a softball. Thousands of reps and mechanical drills honed their skills, and they were highly competent.

Picking up a ball for the first time does not include knowledge of how to throw it. The brain and body are in the unconscious-incapable stage for throwing a ball. At the time of the car accident, for both of my girls, throwing a softball was second nature. They were solidly in the unconscious-capable stage. Yet because of her injuries, Olivia reverted to being unable and unaware of how to throw a softball. She no longer knew how to walk across a room or even how to swallow water. Countless life skills were entirely lost.

WHY AM I WRITING THIS BOOK?

When we reflect on the mission of the church, the central calling is to go make disciples. Over the last twenty plus years, I've had countless conversations with pastors, elders, volunteer leaders, and everyday churchgoers around the topic of disciple making. Yet sadly, those conversations reveal how few of them have ever been intentionally discipled, let alone know how to make a disciple.

This is a tragic deficit—a clear gap between the mission of disciple making and the few people who actually know what disciple making is. I would venture to say that many people in the church today fall in the unconscious-incapable stage when it comes to making disciples. Regardless of the reason, whether a lack of focus, cultural pressures, or an inaccurate definition of winning, they remain unable to carry out the ultimate mission of the church.

Jesus spent three-and-a-half years modeling a methodology to the Twelve. He knew that the mission of reaching the world would be left in the hands of his people, the church. Rather than just teaching truth, Jesus lived in such a way that his followers could see the practical application of truth in everyday life. The Scriptures record Jesus living out this lifestyle and showing his followers how to accomplish the Great Commission. He clearly demonstrated how to make disciples.

From the very beginning when Jesus called his disciples, he stated his intentions to them. One could certainly say that Jesus was unconscious capable at disciple making. For the greatest disciple maker ever to walk the earth, raising up disciples was second nature. It was part of who he is. Jesus taught his disciples to be "fishers of people," his analogy for a disciple who makes disciples. The apostle Paul later used the analogy of being an ambassador. Whether we see ourselves as ambassadors, fishers of people, or disciple makers, the terminology revolves around a central concept: you and I, as disciples of Jesus, are called to go out into the world and, by the power of the Holy Spirit, carry out the mission of making more disciples of Jesus.

How do we discover this ancient art of disciple making? Many Scriptures point to the answer. Paul praised the church in 1 Thessalonians 1:6 for imitating him and his companions as they had imitated Christ. My heart's desire is to help every single Christian move from being unconscious-incapable disciple makers to being unconscious-capable disciple makers—making disciples not because we took a class or our church is running a program but *because that's just who we are*. I want disciple making to become as natural as breathing for every person who follows Jesus.

When Jesus gave us the Great Commission in Matthew 28:18–20, he used the word "go." The Greek context of that term is best translated "as you go." Jesus meant for his church to make disciples as we go about our lives. He meant for us to do it without even thinking about it.

So how can we make making disciples a part of our everyday

lives? How do we move from unconscious incapable to unconscious capable? How do we become people who intentionally make disciples of Jesus as naturally as we take in oxygen? What practices can we learn that equip us to make disciples in our homes, workplaces, churches, and neighborhoods? That's the journey we will travel together in this book. My hope for each of you reading is that by the time you turn the last page over, you will have taken the first step toward disciple making becoming an unconscious-capable skill, a lifestyle that overflows from who you are.

Remember that none of us is perfect. We will have struggles with some practices more than others. That's where grace comes in. We must repeat these practices and live them out in everyday life with the goal of becoming better at making disciples. The process is similar to my daughter's days in rehabilitation as she relearned the basic movements of life. Every day she set goals and took little steps that allowed her to walk, then run, and eventually led her back onto a softball field doing what she loved.

Don't be discouraged. You can do this. It's the vision Jesus has for your life. It's who he is calling you to become. And even though it may require work and you'll need to take some risks, it's not only possible—it's who you were meant to be.

Unconscious capable only comes from thousands of repetitions and often demands discipline and grit to keep from quitting. The life of a disciple maker can never be put into a formula or neat little box. Life is way too messy! For my wife, Amber, and I, watching Olivia work to rehabilitate and reach for her goals brought many days of disappointment, heartache, and concern. Yet other days were filled with tears of joy and triumph. All who dedicate themselves to the ancient path of disciple making will undoubtably experience the same.

At the beginning of her rehab journey, Olivia set a goal to one day play college softball. Four years after the car accident, she realized her dreams when she moved into the dorm as a student athlete, a college softball player. My hope is to inspire you to take up that same attitude and drive to learn and master practices that help you discover and live out the art of intentional, biblical disciple making.

Experience and Apply

Just as Olivia had to practice basic life skills to relearn them in rehab, we must practice the skills associated with intentional disciple making as we seek to move to the unconscious-capable stage. Each chapter of this book includes a story from the Bible that illustrates how the concept from that chapter was modeled by Jesus or another great biblical disciple maker. The story is followed by questions or activities to help you experience and apply what you've read.

You can complete these activities alone, but I would encourage you to work through them with one or two others, or even with a small group (eight to twelve people). Sharing your answers with others always encourages growth, and their answers might give you a different perspective than you've had before. Most importantly, ask God to guide you, and ask him to show you what he wants you to learn or to change as you are becoming an intentional disciple maker.

Consider your life over the past year. Which stage would you say you are currently in when it comes to being a disciple maker?

☐ **Unconscious incapable.** I'm not sure I've ever intentionally discipled anyone, and I don't know where to start. I don't know what I don't know.

☐ **Conscious incapable.** I know that Jesus tells us to make disciples, and I have tried to disciple someone, but I don't think I'm very effective. I think I know what I don't know.

☐ **Conscious capable.** I have a step-by-step plan for making disciples, and I have discipled at least one person. I know what I need to know about discipleship.

☐ **Unconscious capable.** Making disciples is part of my day-to-day life. I have discipled people who have gone on to disciple others. Being an intentional disciple maker is part of who I am. I'm not consciously aware of what I know and how I practice discipleship.

Let's take a look at an example of unconscious-capable disciple making from the New Testament.

Saul was a Jew who persecuted Christians. After a personal encounter with Jesus, he was changed, and his powerful preaching convinced many Jews and Gentiles that Jesus was the Messiah. Saul later became known as Paul.

During Paul's second missionary journey, he and his protégé Silas visited and encouraged the churches that were planted on Paul's first missionary journey. Then Paul had a vision calling him to preach the gospel in Greece, so they sailed to Greece and spent a few days in the Roman colony of Philippi.

In Philippi there was a demon-possessed slave girl who earned money for her masters as a fortune teller. Paul healed the girl, and her masters became very angry because their source of income was taken away. A mob formed against Paul and Silas, and they were beaten severely and thrown in jail. The jailer was ordered to make sure they did not escape.

READ the rest of the story in Acts 16:25–34.

ANSWER these questions:

1. What did Paul and Silas do that had an impact on the jailer?
2. How did these actions cause the jailer to ask how he could be saved?
3. Tell about a time when your actions led someone to ask you about your faith. (If you don't have an answer, what simple changes could you make that would point others to Jesus?)
4. When someone asks about your faith, what will you say?

Paul and Silas were praying and singing to God because that was their usual habit—it's who they were.

When the jailer was distraught, they called out to him and reassured him. Again, that's just who they were. When the jailer asked how to be saved, they told him. They did not have to deeply consider what words to speak or actions to take. Their hearts and minds were aligned with God, and their natural responses resulted in the jailer and his family following Jesus.

PRAY that God will guide you on the path of becoming intentional in your disciple making. Ask him to make it part of who you are so that your words and actions are as effective and glorifying to him as the words and actions of Paul and Silas.

Snapshots

Becoming an Everyday Disciple

BAILEE, A DISCIPLE MAKER

I've never been much of a people person. I have always described myself as a loner girl, an introvert, socially awkward, the quiet type who avoids interaction with others at all costs. I used those phrases to describe myself for my whole life, that is, until I experienced the intentional discipleship and camaraderie that goes on at my church. The first time I walked through the doors, I knew something was different.

People didn't just greet me and move on to the next person; they welcomed me. They stopped what they were doing and took the time to ask me questions about my life. They knew nothing about me, but they actually cared to learn about me. But it didn't stop there. People reached out to me at random times throughout the week to check on me, ask if I needed prayer, ask if I had found a small group to plug into, or ask if I could meet for lunch. At first I thought it was the weirdest thing, and I wondered who these crazy people were who kept pestering me. I kept everyone at an arm's distance and didn't really want to reciprocate the kindness being shown to me.

A few months later, I realized that I had heard the message about discipleship over and over again, like a resounding gong. Week after week, message after message, our pastor preached about discipleship—I was so tired of it! I did not understand what the big deal was or why this church kept going over it time and time again. First off, I didn't even know what that fancy word meant, so I had to google it and ask around. What I learned is that the definition of *discipleship* is walking alongside someone to help that person follow Jesus, be changed by Jesus, and be on mission for Jesus. But at the time, I didn't feel like anyone was intentionally discipling me. My past hurts and struggles led me to believe that I must have slipped through the cracks, that no one cared about me, that I wasn't good enough to be "discipled." Little did I realize that those people who were pestering me throughout the week, calling and texting me, checking on me, and never giving up on helping me feel welcomed were creating exactly the relational environment that I didn't know I needed but desperately craved.

Once I finally came to the end of myself, surrendered my heart to God, and truly accepted the love these people were showing me, I saw things in a new light. I allowed people into my heart and my life, which led to conversations about being discipled. I asked an amazing, strong, kindhearted woman of God to disciple me and walk alongside me in my journey with Jesus, and she graciously accepted. She has stood by my side for the last year, our arms linked together in a beautiful relationship where she speaks truth with love and grace. She gently guides and corrects me, and she prays fervently with me.

This woman's plan in discipling me in the beginning was clear yet very simple. It was to walk beside me in all that I was going through, praying with me and for me, and modeling how to live a godly life. It was to help me move closer to Jesus and to become more like him every day so that one day I would be able to disciple and love others. She loved me. So now I do not describe myself as a loner girl who avoids people. Through the intentional love and discipleship that this woman modeled for me, I describe myself as a Jesus-loving disciple maker who intentionally makes disciples.

Rather than walk through a lobby with my head down, I walk with my eyes up, looking for that woman just like me. Every day I do my best to follow Christ in the power of the Holy Spirit and be that disciple he calls me to be. No more googling definitions, my life is now committed to his mission, and I understand what it means to live this mission rather than just read about it.

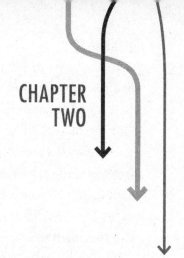

LISTEN WITH THE INTENT TO UNDERSTAND

Teaching through translation can be difficult. Over the past twenty years, I've had the opportunity to speak on disciple making in many different countries, and I've found that when speaking through a translator, words and definitions become critical. In some countries, I've used words in English that do not translate very well into the local language. Misunderstandings have forced me to clarify my thoughts and my language.

Rarely do I speak about disciple making without using the term *intentional*. Yet this is one of those words that sometimes requires a more thorough explanation. I typically define *intentional* as "being purposeful or deliberate." And when we study the life of Christ and truly understand his call to go and make disciples, we begin to see that the process of disciple making

15

requires intentionality—purposeful, deliberate, and conscious choices and actions every step of the way.

Regardless of where we live or what languages we speak, we cannot effectively make a disciple without being intentional. And one of the practices that is critical for intentional disciple making—a practice that may be a purposeful and deliberate choice for many of us—is the practice of listening to others with the intent to understand.

Typically I take Friday as my day off. One Friday I stood in our kitchen around 3:30 p.m. I remember the time because I heard my daughter, Olivia, who was nine years old at the time, come through the front door as she arrived home from school. Normally when Olivia comes through the door, you know it's her by the loud and energetic personality God gave her. But this day was different. There were no rays of vibrant sunshine on that day. Instead, a storm cloud of frustration burst into the living room. I could hear the sound of sniffles mixed with rumbling grunts, then a backpack hit the floor with a thud, and a nine-year-old body flopped onto the couch. Clearly something was wrong.

I stepped from our kitchen to the living room to uncover the problem.

"What's wrong, Olivia?" I asked.

Red circles surrounded her eyes, and she was choking back tears. In frustrated disgust, Olivia began to tell me how her older sister, Emma, who was twelve, hit her in the arm on their way up the driveway after the school bus dropped them off. Before Olivia could finish the story, her accused older sister walked through the door.

I could tell that she, too, had been crying, and she immediately began to justify why she had thrown a punch. I felt my blood pressure start to rise, and I inhaled sharply, preparing to unload the typical parental response to this kind of situation. *Pause the story.* If you are a parent with two or more kids who are old enough to fight, wrestle, or take a swing at each other, you know what I wanted to ask my oldest daughter: "Why did you hit your sister?"

That moment in my living room taught me more about disciple making than almost any other single event in life. At the time, I was studying how to ask good, healthy questions. Listening with the intent to understand was a new concept in my life, and at just that moment God gave me his awareness. I knew that I had to change my question. I needed to apply what I was learning. In similar situations in the past, I would have fired out the question, "Why?" I would have demanded that my older daughter give me some feasible reason for hitting her sister. "Justify to me, twelve-year-old, *why* you hit your younger sister!"

But I didn't. Instead, I changed the question, and it changed me. Rather than asking and listening to my older daughter, Emma, in a way that drove my response, I chose to listen to her with curiosity to help me understand. Emma's behavior was a bit untypical, and I could tell that she was pretty upset, so I stopped, took a breath, and changed my approach.

I asked Emma to sit next to me on the couch. I looked her in the eyes, knowing that something else was going on. I asked, "What happened today that upset you?"

Emma slumped her shoulders, hung her head, and through tears told me about how some kids had teased her earlier in the day. They had made fun of her and embarrassed her. She went on to tell me that when Olivia asked her about it after school, Emma told her to stop. But Olivia persisted. So out of frustration, Emma slugged her in the shoulder. Olivia became the target of Emma's expression of hurt and anger.

Were Emma's actions wrong? Yes. Did I understand more of the situation? Yes. And the more I listened and repeated back to her what I was hearing, the more she opened up about other teasing that was going on. She also told me that she and a longtime friend at school were no longer friends. That is a big deal to a twelve-year-old. Emma opened her heart to me and shared pain that ran deeper than an exchange between two sisters in a driveway. I was able to hear her story, understand her perspective, and minister to her heart.

I then asked what she thought she needed to do about her sister. I watched as Emma, on her own accord, got up and hugged her sister and offered a heartfelt apology. I saw genuine reconciliation, and I was closer to my daughter after the conflict than before. I could minister to her about some real issues she was battling at school. But had I followed the typical, worn trail I often traveled in these situations, I would have missed what was really happening, the heart-level, deeper issues at play.

LISTENING TO UNDERSTAND

Most of us are terrible listeners. In most conversations, and especially in heated conversations, we listen with the goal of responding. We prepare our next comeback or defend our position. We abandon curiosity about other people's positions, and we load our verbal guns. We respond to prove them wrong or convince them to believe they are wrong. The truth is, all of us naturally listen to respond. It's just "who we are."

And the reason is very simple: we are selfish. When my girls came through the front door upset, I just wanted the problem resolved. In my flesh, I wanted the fighting to stop and peace to return to our home. I did not prioritize understanding the root of the problem. I love my kids and do not want them to fight, but if I'm honest, my core motivations are almost always about me—my comfort, my peace, my preferences and desires.

Think about a time when you've been frustrated with or offended by someone, especially a spouse or child. Typically our immediate response is a question or statement that demands justification of their behavior. And when two individuals speak from their own perspectives, they are responding out of their own brokenness. The problem is that we only clearly hear the pieces that help us better defend ourselves in response. We master the art of building our defense, not understanding what might be going on with the other person. Listening to respond sets the table for such hostile interactions.

IT'S NOT ABOUT YOU

Being successful in *intentional* disciple making requires listening well. We must intentionally shift from what is natural and normal and listen to understand, not just respond. To do this, we must set aside our own agendas. Listening to understand means getting ourselves out of the way and frees us to focus on what is truly being said. One of the most profound realizations I made that day in the living room with my daughters was that this situation was not about me. The core of the story was my daughter's struggles at school, magnified by a pesky little sister.

By getting out of the way and listening with the intent to understand, I learned what was most important to Emma. When I shifted from demanding justification *of* her actions to curiosity *about* her actions, the entire conversation changed. Even though hitting her sister was not acceptable, the truth was exposed when I stepped out of the way and listened to her story. She felt heard and made the relational corrections that were needed.

Now think about Jesus. Of any human being who ever walked the face of the earth, he had every right in every situation to make it "all about him." Yet countless times he asked questions and listened to the responses of those around him. He is God, and although he knows the thoughts and motives of every heart, the Gospels record him asking more than three hundred questions. He consistently and constantly modeled for his disciples how important it is to listen with the intent to understand. Jesus not only wanted to hear the hearts of those he discipled but also wanted them to practice this kind of listening themselves.

Listening well to others communicates that we care for them and want to know more about them. A more thorough understanding of the one we are speaking with unlocks deeper relationship and opens the door for us to live out many of the other practices of intentional disciple making. Author David Augsburger captures this concept well: "Being heard is so close to being loved that, for the average person, they are almost indistinguishable."[1]

PRINCIPLES OF THE PRACTICE

Listening to understand helps us know the hearts of the people we are discipling, but we must also help them practice listening themselves. I have heard people share remarkable stories of pain, loss, success, and triumph. These stories tend to come out when the focus is on understanding rather than becoming caught up in formulating a response.

So how do we learn this unnatural skill? Below are five key principles we can employ with the intent of listening to understand.

Follow the Other Person's Story

Over the years, I have engaged with many different individuals across a table and listened as they shared stories about their lives. Frequently, at the end of those encounters, I have said very little. They often say things like, "Wow! Talking with you today was so helpful!" I just smile, not because of the compliment, but because I am witnessing the positive impact of people feeling heard and encouraged simply because I was quiet and listened. I rarely give advice or share my opinion on the topic being discussed, yet often they thank me for helping them or express how much they appreciate my input. What each one is really saying is thank you for listening to my story without interrupting me. Thank you for loving me by hearing me.

Like bread crumbs along a trail, we all drop key words or truths that are important to our stories. When we remain disciplined in following others' stories without inserting elements of our own stories, people feel valued and heard.

Practice intentionally following along by paying close attention to the details. Repeat their spoken words back to them and follow the bread crumbs they leave. In this way, we draw closer to the individual because we know their story better. We meet the human need to be known. Listening well builds trust and creates relational security. We have cared enough to hear and understand without judgment, fixing, or derailing the conversation by injecting our own story.

Imagine that we are sitting together and you tell me that you just took a vacation. I follow along by replying, "Oh, wow! You went on vacation—tell me more about it." You continue by saying that during your vacation you had a powerful quiet time with God, and you really connected with him. I would say something like, "What I am hearing you say is that you had an incredible time with God." You go on to say that the restful time you had was awesome, and even the food you ate was as if it were manna from heaven. I might say something like, "So the trip was restful, but tell me more about this manna from heaven. What was this food you ate?"

I use your words and follow your story. I choose not to cut you off by telling you about my morning devotions or what I had for breakfast. I don't offer my opinion on the most restful place to vacation. I simply listen to and follow *your story*. When I take the time to listen to your words and speak them back to you, you feel heard. And as you hear your own words spoken back to you, your brain responds. Sometimes you might correct me or adjust the story. The critical point is that I am focused on you, not me, and you are feeling heard because I listened.

Remove Your Agenda

To hear another's story well and listen with the intent to understand, you must set aside your agenda. When Olivia came through the door that day after school and I could see how upset she was, I just wanted to fix the problem. My agenda was to deal with the problem as swiftly and cleanly as possible—to solve it and move on with the day. When Emma came through the door, I had to fight intentionally against my own agenda and the urge to put my emotions at the center of the story. I set my agenda aside and became curious about what had happened that caused her to act so out of character. Resisting the urge to make the conversation about me and my agenda allowed me to ask questions to better understand.

So how do you set aside your agenda? In a practical sense, you take an inventory of the conversation and ask yourself some questions. Is the person you are talking to asking for your ideas or input? Is this person seeking your counsel or just sharing their heart? When you converse with someone you are discipling, and they are sharing about their life or a difficult situation, refrain from sharing all the great advice you want to give and simply focus on that person. Remember that it's not about you; it's about the other person feeling heard.

Listening with the intent to understand allows you to set aside your agenda and hear someone fully. The agenda you have might be helpful, healthy, or even the right solution to their problem, but without first listening well, you risk stifling the conversation. Think about people in your life who come to you with an agenda and rarely listen to you.

It's frustrating, isn't it? Learn to set aside your agenda, follow the other person's story, and watch what happens to the depth of the conversation.

Abandon the Need to Be Right

No one likes to be around someone who thinks they are always right. We often have different perspectives than the people with whom we are speaking. When we listen with the intent to understand, sometimes we need to set aside our need to be right. Wow! That can be hard to do. Just like tabling our agendas, sometimes we also need to set our "rightness" to the side. Trying to convince someone why we are right can become exhausting in a conversation, and it will almost certainly kill any curiosity we might have about a person's story. When we insist on being right, people will feel manipulated and not heard.

Let me share an example from a conversation I had with a man named Jarred. Jarred aspired to become a world-famous musician. When he shared his story, I followed along and learned that Jarred had made many attempts at stardom, only to find himself coming up short every time. Now swamped with debt and no stable job on the horizon, he was struggling. He was married with two young children and barely making ends meet with a few side jobs. Yet Jarred refused to give up his dreams at the expense of paying everyday bills. His life was falling apart, and I could see that unless he quickly made some changes, things were going to spiral out of control.

As I listened, everything in me wanted to stop Jarred, give him advice, and tell him what he clearly needed to do—except . . . that is *not* what Jarred needed. Jarred needed to share his entire story with me. He needed me to understand. He was not ready to make any changes, nor was he even asking for my opinion. So I just sat in the *hard* with him. I listened with the intent to understand, waiting for any opportunity he might give me to speak truth. I patiently waited on the Holy Spirit to open the door for Jarred to be receptive to the truth I could see and for him to solicit my input.

A week later, Jarred did come to me and ask for advice. I shared my ideas with him and even spoke truth to him. I said that maybe it was time to give up the pursuit of a record label and, at least for now, find a job so that he could provide for his family. His story turned out well in the end. Jarred still dabbles in music, but he also has a great-paying job and is able to support his family.

We can create countless scenarios where we would be justified in telling someone who is wrong why we are right. I get it. And to be clear, I am not talking about life-and-death situations or times when a poor decision could lead to extreme danger. What I am talking about are the vast number of conversations we have when we are discipling people struggling with life issues. When we so badly want to tell them why we are right and why what they are doing is wrong. It's far better if we instead follow their stories, remove our agendas, set aside the need to be right, and just listen.

Stay Curious

Woven throughout the previous three principles is a characteristic critical to the art of listening well: you must stay *curious* about the other person. When the other person is telling their story, remind yourself that the conversation is not about you. Put those selfish tendencies to death and focus on the person with whom you are interacting.

When I sat on the couch with Emma, she needed me to be curious about her day. That was my only hope of discovering what was really lurking below the surface. At first I saw the surface level—that she lashed out at her sister—but when I remained curious and asked questions, the hurt that was hiding came into the light.

Remain curious with those you are discipling. When you do, you'll learn wonderful things about others, and they will feel safer sharing with you. Jesus is God, and he knew the intentions of those around him, yet he still modeled an attitude of curiosity. You can, too, and it will help you to be intentional in your disciple making.

Avoid "One-Upping"

I get excited when I hear others share stories or talk about the important events in their lives. I love to tell old hunting stories and share about the great things going on in my own life. But nothing shuts me down faster when I am telling a story than someone else interrupting with these words: "Yeah, that's a great story, but *you should have seen what happened to me. . . .*" One-upping occurs more than we realize. Even good-hearted people do it, just wanting to relate to others. But negatively it shuts people down.

Unfortunately, I've seen well-intentioned people one-up someone who is going through extreme pain in an effort to relate. Whether in uplifting or painful stories, I strongly caution against one-upping statements. When you intention-ally disciple someone, you are focused on that person. Take yourself out of the picture. Sure, the conversation may naturally turn and provide an opportunity for you to share about your own life, but when someone is sharing their own story or open-ing up about their own experience, follow that person's story, drop your agenda, and lay down your need to be the center of attention. Maintain a mindset of curiosity, learning all you can to create genuine care for that person. This intentional focus will often eliminate the temptation to one-up someone when they are telling their story.

The practice of listening to understand must be seasoned with grace. We all forget this at times and inevitably insert our agenda. So resist the urge to beat yourself up. These prac-tices take time to learn, and like any new skill, they must be repeated again and again before they become strong habits. Remember, this is a lifestyle we commit to, not a legalistic set of rules.

Intentional disciple making is an art. Listening to under-stand becomes a skill that you and I attempt to live out, know-ing full well that sometimes we will mess up. I still become impatient at times and share my own agenda or fail to follow a story. I have also shared my story at the wrong time in an attempt to relate. We are human, but each of us is given a clear plan from Jesus on how to walk out the life of an intentional disciple maker. Start each day by listening to the Holy Spirit and asking him to help you better understand others. Watch as he responds by showing you how to be a better listener—and a better disciple maker.

Experience and Apply →

Think about some of the conversations you have been involved in recently. Based on those conversations, evaluate your listening skills by answering these questions TRUE or FALSE:

1. I am able to complete a conversation without my emotions causing me to direct the conversation a certain way. _____

2. I do not ask that the other person justify their actions to me. _____

3. I can listen to someone else talk without forming a response in my mind. _____

4. I have been told that I am a good listener. _____

5. I am comfortable in a conversation where I speak 25 percent or less of the time. _____

6. I do not enter most conversations with a goal in mind. _____

7. People ask me to help them talk through difficult topics. _____

8. I do not feel the need to "win" a conversation. _____

9. I rarely voice my opinion about the topic being discussed. _____

10. No one has walked away from a conversation with me recently. _____

If you answered FALSE to three or more of these questions, your listening skills could use a tune-up.

Let's explore a story where Jesus asked questions to help him better understand his disciples.

At the beginning of Matthew 16, Jesus taught the disciples that the Pharisees and Sadducees were deceptive in their teaching, and the disciples should be careful not to be taken in by their deceit. This account follows that conversation.

READ the story in Matthew 16:13–20.

ANSWER these questions:

1. What is the first question Jesus asked?
2. How did that question set the stage for the conversation that followed?
3. Simon Peter responded to the next question. What did his response reveal to Jesus, and to us, about Peter's faith?
4. How can we use this story today to begin intentional conversations with those around us?

By asking who people said he was, Jesus required the disciples to think about what they had heard and consider how other people's estimation of him matched or differed from their own experiences with him. Notice that Jesus did not respond to their answers. He did not confirm or deny what they had said. Jesus then asked them to consider a personal assessment of who they thought he was.

Peter's immediate response, "You are the Messiah, the Son of the living God," revealed that Peter's faith was solid and that he was committed to the mission.

PRACTICE listening to understand. Think of someone in your sphere of influence who is not close to Jesus. Make plans to have coffee or a meal with that person this week, and during your time together ask, "Who do you think Jesus is?" Set aside your agenda. Surrender your need to be right. Do not refute or challenge any answer. Repeat back what you hear the person say to verify that you hear correctly. Let the person hear their own words restated. You may ask clarifying questions, but mostly *just listen.*

(Note: It is best not to practice this skill on close friends or family members with whom you have emotional ties. When you have more experience with listening to understand, the skill is effective with everyone.)

PRAY that the Holy Spirit will use the conversation to open doors of communication where the discussion can go deeper. Ask him to help you trust him more fully as you listen without responding. Ask that he would open your eyes to the path of faith your friend is walking and give you future opportunities to speak truth into that person's life.

LISA, A DISCIPLE MAKER

One Sunday morning I was standing in the church lobby when a woman came out of the worship service, found a tissue, and sat on a chair sobbing quietly. I went to sit by her to see if I could help. She continued weeping as she explained that her husband had recently left. She and her teenage children were struggling emotionally and financially. I offered to help her find a Christian counselor, but she asked if I would meet with her. I was taken aback. I had no training as a counselor. We arranged a day and time to meet together later that week. I recall thinking that meeting would give me more time to convince her to see a licensed counselor.

We met at my office where we could talk privately. She spent nearly an hour telling me about the difficult season she was experiencing. I had moved out from behind my desk, and I sat in a chair facing her. My phone was silenced, and my attention was focused on her story. I had tissues ready for the inevitable tears, and I waited patiently as she regained her composure time and time again. Throughout her story, I nodded, asked clarifying questions, and tried to stay right with her as she recounted a heartbreaking story of the loss of her marriage and some of her lifelong dreams.

I understood her pain, having experienced a similar loss

myself, several months earlier. There were moments when I was tempted to sympathize by sharing part of my story, but I refrained. I had previously attended a listening workshop where we were taught not to insert our story into a conversation like this.

When the woman had run out of words or tears, or maybe both, she stopped talking and looked up at me with a look of relief on her face. She said, "Oh my goodness. I feel so much better! You are wonderful!" I was tempted to look around and see if she was speaking to someone else, but I knew we were alone in my office. I had barely said ten words since our time together began. How could that have possibly helped? Nevertheless, I smiled and told her I was glad she felt encouraged. I was about to suggest that counselor I had in mind for her when she asked if I would meet with her again the next week. She told me that our time together was more helpful than anything had been since her trial had begun. We prayed together and set an appointment for the following week.

When she left my office, I sat and contemplated what I might have said or done that was particularly helpful. I had just listened to her. I finally realized that is what she needed— someone to really listen to her story and how the events had affected her. As she spoke and heard her own words, her brain began to organize and process the events she had experienced. That gave her the capacity to move forward in the next steps she needed to take. She felt that she could now make it through the next few days.

We continued to meet weekly for several months, and she processed different aspects of her new life with me. I listened and occasionally asked questions, and eventually I was able to infuse truth from Scripture when I could see a spot where her belief system was broken. We developed a relationship in which I was later able to share parts of my story and we could process single life together in a healthy way.

There is definitely a time and a place for professional counseling, but there is also great value in a friend who will intentionally listen to understand. You may be surprised by how much progress someone can make if you take time to focus on that person and just listen!

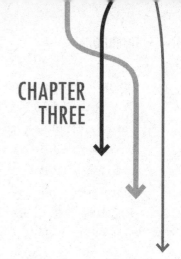

SEEK THE HOLY SPIRIT

When our girls played fast-pitch softball, I hated sitting in the stands. I became so nervous watching them play that I felt better standing. So I would watch the game standing a short distance from the bleachers, often pacing around. Yes, I was *that* dad, and this was especially true when my daughter Emma was pitching. To manage my excitement and anxiety, I found it best to stand a little farther back from the action. I may have feared verbalizing my thoughts and having other people hear them, but whatever the reason, I found that standing back a bit from the crowd had some unexpected benefits. I could easily survey what was going on, not only in the game but by watching the parents around me. During those tense moments of pacing back and forth or in between innings, I met other dads and struck up conversations. Some of them were quite powerful.

I remember one of those games, a hot and humid summer

day in Houston, when Emma was playing in a tournament. During the course of the tournament, I noticed a man who was often standing back away from the crowd. His daughter was new to our team, and he always stood alone. He was tall and thin with dark sunglasses—nothing unusual about his appearance. Sporting a farmer's tan, his face was locked in a perpetual look of concern, his foot propped up on a small Igloo cooler. I figured his daughter probably stored her tournament snacks in there. Well, my intentional disciple-making bells started clanging, and I decided I wanted to know his story.

Between innings of one of the games, I walked up and introduced myself. We did the typical dad thing and talked about who our daughters were and what positions they played. We discussed the strengths of the team and how much we enjoyed watching them play. The man's name was Jay, and over the weekend Jay and I continued to talk. I asked questions with the intention of understanding who he was. And for the rest of that tournament, we talked about life and got to know each other better.

As summer passed, Jay and I continued to see each other at different softball tournaments. And in between tournaments, I found myself praying for Jay. I asked God to show me what Jay was looking for and to give me the words to say when I saw him the next time. I prayed for Jay's salvation and surrendered myself to the Holy Spirit's direction, asking him to use me however he wanted to reach Jay for Christ.

Whenever I saw Jay, I asked God to give me the right words and to help me to be sensitive to what God was already doing in Jay's life. I wanted to stay in a posture of listening to understand—but also having eyes to watch and see where

God was at work in this relationship. I continued to learn more about Jay, that he had an older son serving in the army, he loved deep-sea fishing, and he hated green Gatorade.

As we become unconscious-capable disciple makers, we must remember that God goes before us, already at work. And God is also *for* us, ready to support and come alongside our meager efforts if we do them in faith and ask for his help. We'll engage in spiritual conversations, and some will be clear and powerful. Others might feel cloudier and seem insignificant. We might wonder about God's timing, but if we are patient, we never have to guess if God is working. God is *always* at work.

After nearly an entire summer and dozens of conversations, I began to assume that Jay and I would never talk about the Lord. I had dropped a few hints along the way. I had mentioned that I would miss Sunday games because of attending church. I brought up the small group I was leading, but Jay never engaged me on that. He usually just nodded or said nothing. But I continued to pray, seek, and wait for God to move rather than force an answer to a question Jay did not seem to have. Then one day, as the summer tournament season was drawing to a close, Jay spoke up.

Between innings of a game, he asked me about God. He already knew I was a pastor from our first conversation when I shared what I did for a living. And though we had never talked about it before, Jay now began asking questions about God and about church. To my delight, behind those sunglasses and under that faded Astros hat, God was working. Jay opened up that day, sharing with me some painful events in his life. He confessed to me that he had never darkened the doors of a church. Jay had no idea what it meant to have a relationship with Christ. And right there before my eyes, I could see what God was doing; the Holy Spirit was drawing Jay to salvation in Christ. I silently sought God in that moment, listened to understand Jay, and watched God do what only he can do.

Jay had no idea that I had been praying for him and watching for opportunities to intentionally invest spiritual truth in his life. He was unaware that God was at work and drawing him closer to relationship with Christ. My motivation in all this was not to put another notch in my Bible or improve a statistic for our church. God put Jay right in front of me while the two of us stood and watched our daughters play softball. I simply wanted to be available for God, grow closer to Jay, and in that moment, do my best as God's ambassador.

The Lord works this way—all the time. We just need to be willing to watch for his working and set ourselves up to be ready to take the next step when he says go. Following the model of Christ means adhering to his timing. Sometimes Jesus pauses to point out an issue or provide a spiritual prompting. We must also learn to pause and look to see what he is doing. This requires patience as we wait on God to move or work.

A PURPOSEFUL PAUSE

Seeking the leading of God's Spirit is not always easy. I was discussing the discipline of seeking the Holy Spirit with my friend Shelly, the women's discipleship coordinator on our church staff, and I shared with her that I often become impatient with God and his timing. She then told me that the Lord had recently taught her a concept called the *purposeful pause*. As we seek to be intentional with ourselves and our own walk with Christ, sometimes we must give ourselves permission to wait and be patient. We must allow space for a pause, a purposeful time of waiting, as part of our daily walk. Rather than spiritually tapping a foot while waiting on God to give us the green light, we can pause patiently, knowing there is intention behind the pause.

Since our lives are often busy and filled with distractions, a pause opens the door for God to focus our attention where he desires and allows the Holy Spirit to work. Pausing gives us an opportunity to notice what God is doing. Slowing down and focusing on him requires intentionality, and in that space, God will often show us the next steps to take. But this doesn't always come naturally. For us to hear God and take full advantage of the purposeful pause, we must implement some principles that can help us *seek the Holy Spirit*.

PRINCIPLES OF THE PRACTICE

In both high school and college, I worked construction for my dad. We built all kinds of buildings, from apartments to strip malls, and worked on duplexes and single-family homes. One summer we even built a movie theater. The variety of buildings gave me an opportunity to work on almost every phase of construction. Regardless of the building project, every morning we put on our tool belts, and no matter the job that day, we always equipped ourselves with some of the same tools.

As we seek God by living out his call to intentional disciple making, we need to know that we have tools as well. These may not be the kind of tools you would normally think of, though.

Certainly we must read our Bibles and utilize commentaries, devotionals, and other resources to help us grow in our Christian journey, but I want you to think about other tools that are critical yet used regularly by only a few. These tools are more intangible yet vital to the disciple-making process. When used properly, they help us intentionally build the kingdom of God. They are the tools of *abiding in Christ, prayer and fasting, being patient,* and *focusing on truth.* I have found these four tools to be essential whenever I'm seeking God to be more intentional with those I disciple.

Abiding in Christ

Thinking of abiding in Christ as a tool may seem unusual, but it's as essential to the work of disciple making as a hammer is to building. After all, what is a carpenter without a hammer? In a similar way, how can we possibly make disciples of Christ if we are not abiding in Christ?

When we abide in Christ, we draw closer to our Master. Abiding, when practiced habitually, helps us grow as disciples. As we abide, we hear Christ's instructions for daily living and gain the courage, empowerment, and direction essential for our own intentional disciple making. The process of abiding that Jesus describes in John 15 is not complicated. It's about each of us remaining in the vine—Jesus—as he gives us what we need. And Jesus identifies our need. Hear what he says in John 15:4–5: "Remain in me, as I also remain in you. No branch can bear fruit by itself; it must remain in the vine. Neither can you bear fruit unless you remain in me. I am the vine; you are the branches. If you remain in me and I in you, you will bear much fruit; apart from me you can do nothing."

Abiding is about more than reading your Bible or a morning devotional verse, although those are important and part of abiding. But it's easy for us to focus on what we *do*. The abiding I am talking about is not only something we do; it is an extension of who we are, our identity. It's as natural and normal as seeing a carpenter with a hammer in his hand or hanging from his belt. Abiding describes the way God wants to relate to us. It's the kind of relationship God has wanted with humans since the garden of Eden. Abiding goes beyond checking boxes and doing our religious duty. It's taking up a tool that shapes who we are, changing us to be more like Christ as we come alongside him in his work of building the kingdom of God one life at a time.

So what does it mean to abide? Ask yourself a few questions. *Am I spending time with God in a way that is relational and life giving? Do I think of my time with the Lord as a thing to do or as a chance to catch up with a friend? Do I find myself reading the Bible just to check a religious box on my task list? Do I spend time with God for a few minutes and then go about my day without him, or do I spend time throughout the day talking to him and drawing close?* Maybe for you, abiding in Christ is going for a walk and talking with him. Abiding may look like singing a song while doing a household chore or quietly reflecting while journaling.

Prayer and Fasting

In addition to abiding in Christ, another tool that hangs from the belt of an intentional disciple maker is prayer and fasting. If abiding is our hammer, I see prayer and fasting as a pry bar. Most any person in the construction industry has a multi-tool on their belt for pulling nails, lifting lids from paint cans, or breaking loose something that's stuck. Prayer and fasting are the pry bars or multi-tools of disciple making.

But whereas a carpenter will often use a pry bar dozens of times every day on a jobsite, we sometimes forget that we have this spiritual tool of prayer and fasting. Life can get so hectic that we forget about the power of these biblical practices. Using them doesn't even cross our minds. Note that the prayer I'm talking about here is not the same kind of prayer we talked about previously with abiding. That kind of prayer is about seeking a deeper relationship with Jesus, more of a conversation between friends. This type of prayer shifts the focus off of us and petitions God to move in the life of another person, breaking things loose in the person's life.

When I was spending that time at tournaments talking with Jay, I continued to pray for God to show me what Jay would need, the words to say to him. At different points along the way, in my devotions and quiet times with God, I prayed for Jay and sought God for him specifically. Many times I fasted—refraining from eating for a time to help focus my prayers. That was when I began to see that God was really working on Jay, and soon afterword Jay began to ask questions about God. My time of abiding in Christ led me to fast, and I spent two days fasting and praying for Jay to find salvation in Christ. During that fast, I prayed for the hardness of Jay's heart to be broken and spiritual bonds to be loosened. I began to step up, interceding before the Lord for him.

When we utilize the tools of prayer and fasting, we may find ourselves in a place like I did at the softball game where I first met Jay. That first day I met him, I looked over and saw a man standing by himself, and the Holy Spirit did what he does: he gave me a distinct sense that I needed to go talk to that man. Looking back, I'm convinced that interaction came about because a day or two beforehand I had been praying and fasting, asking God who he wanted me to disciple. By taking the tool of prayer and fasting off my tool belt and putting it into practice, God used my obedience to bring Jay into my life. Jay eventually joined my small group and came to our church, and several months later I had the joy of leading Jay to Christ and baptizing him. All of this came from seeking the Lord, using the tools he has provided for making disciples.

I ask you to consider these questions: *Have you spent time in prayer, asking God to give you someone to disciple intentionally? Have you fasted and sought the Lord for answers on who to disciple or how to do it? When was the last time you spent the better part of a day in prayer for a potential disciple?* God gave us a specific job to do, and he gave us these tools for a purpose. Jesus even modeled how and when to use them. It's up to us to take the tool of prayer and fasting off the belt and get to work.

Being Patient

Another essential tool on the construction worker's tool belt is the measuring tape. Full disclosure: I dislike this tool when doing construction work because I have trouble hooking the end on right. Just before I get the exact measurement I need, the tape inevitably snaps back at me. That's why when I think of the measuring tape, I think of patience. If you want your work to turn out right, you need to patiently utilize the measuring tape to get accurate measurements—even if the process takes time. Likewise, when we seek God in our efforts to make disciples, we must utilize the tool of patience. Don't rush, or you will sabotage the job. God rarely moves at the speed we expect or desire him to move. Measuring off our next steps requires that we wait on God to do his part and take our cue from him as to what comes next.

When we become impatient and get ahead of God, we are much like a builder who fails to take proper measurements. Imagine rushing through the process of building a set of stairs by eyeballing the measurements and then quickly making your cuts. If you don't attempt accuracy and never take a measurement, you end up wasting time, energy, and expensive materials. Construction workers have a common saying: "Measure twice; cut once." In the same way, when we remain patient, we end up with the results God wants. Sometimes God may move quickly, but in my experience with disciple making, God's ways are often precise, methodical, and frequently slower than I desire.

I often create deadlines in my mind, and then I think God should operate from this unspoken timeline. If I do not see the fruit I have been praying for, I assume I must be doing something wrong. The tool of patience gives us permission to slow down and make sure what we are doing is in step with what God is doing. We align ourselves to him, not the other way around. Too often we bring in our agendas; we want to see those we've been praying for come to Christ immediately. However, it might take years for someone to come to Christ. Remember that God is in charge, and it is the work of the Holy Spirit to which we are surrendered. So wait . . . be patient. Let God work.

Now ask yourself another set of questions. *Am I being impatient with those around me as it relates to spiritual matters? How am I putting my desires or agenda ahead of God's timing? Can I better help someone I am discipling by slowing down and waiting on God to work?*

Focusing on Truth

Though I regularly used all the tools in my tool belt at different times, there was one tool I needed in every facet of building. I carried around a small level about eight inches in length, using it to check any wall or tabletop we were building, constantly making sure things were flush. When we are intentionally discipling someone, truth is the level. And this truth comes only from the Word of God.

I have found myself in many conversations that, even as I think of them now, were pretty incredible. I've listened to people share about broken beliefs and difficult pain, and I've seen lies and misunderstandings brought into the light during discipling conversations. When I seek God for direction and weave that into listening to understand, powerful things happen. The Holy Spirit convicts and draws out the lies people believe. I find that I must intentionally focus on the truth of God's Word to guide me in these conversations. Truth gives me a plumb line to put up against whatever is said to see if it is actually on the level, or true.

When putting a level on a wall, we watch to see how close the bubble is to the center. We do the same when we listen to what people say, checking that against biblical truth. And this next part is critical: when listening, we will hear people's brokenness, but *we must resist the urge to jump in and fix it in that moment.* Even as we hear their pain and hurt and recognize brokenness, we must still earn the right to speak truth into their lives.

Let's go back to my story about Jay again. During one of our conversations, Jay shared with me something he believed about God—something that was the opposite of what Scripture says. He said, "God doesn't really care about my problems, so I have no reason to tell him about my life." Hundreds, if not thousands, of Scripture verses refute that lie. Yet in that moment, Jay was pouring out his heart to me, and I knew I needed to be quiet and listen. I hoped God would give me an opportunity to share truth, but I was still earning Jay's trust, and I knew that trust would later allow me to bring in the "level" of biblical truth. Several hours later, as our conversation carried on, God opened a door for that, and I asked Jay's permission to share about who I knew God to be. I put that level against the cracked foundation of Jay's belief, he received it, and we were able to press forward into deeper discussion.

In this case, being able to focus on God's truth happened in a matter of hours, but this doesn't always happen. Sometimes it takes months or even years to be able to speak truth into a person's broken beliefs or lies. This is where patience comes in, where prayer and fasting are applied, and where we must live out the habit of abiding in Christ. The tool of focusing on truth demonstrates why intentional disciple making is an art. It flows from a lifestyle that goes beyond any program or list that we can follow. My relationship with Jay is a success story, but other relationships haven't been so successful. Unfortunately, I have other stories that turned out very differently from Jay's. In those relationships, no matter how much I listened or shared truth, those people still rejected what I had to say and, in some cases, severed their ties with me entirely.

Seeking the Holy Spirit is an essential practice in intentional disciple making. Sometimes doing so is difficult to describe and at other times it is confusing. But when seeking the Holy Spirit becomes a natural practice, unconscious capable, we can experience the most amazingly rewarding moments we will ever have this side of heaven. Seeing Jay surrender his life to Christ, be baptized, and follow Jesus as a disciple reminds me of why I do what I do.

Experience and Apply →

Use this scale to evaluate your personal abiding time with God, and respond to each statement:

Never—1   Seldom—2   Occasionally—3   Frequently—4   Always—5

_____   1. I regularly (five to six times per week) read and study the Bible and look forward to that time with Christ.

_____   2. When the Bible exposes an area of my life needing change, I respond with repentance and do my part to make things right with God and others.

_____   3. I replace impure or inappropriate thoughts with God's truth from Scripture.

_____   4. I evaluate cultural ideas and lifestyles by biblical standards.

_____   5. My prayers include thanksgiving, praise, confession, requests, and listening.

_____   6. I understand and practice the discipline of biblical fasting.

_____ 7. I trust God to answer when I pray and wait patiently on his timing.

_____ 8. I cooperate with the Holy Spirit throughout the day, with purposeful pauses to inquire of where the heavenly Father is working.

_____ 9. I seek godly counsel and appreciate correction from other mature believers.

_____ 10. I expect to grow in my faith journey as a follower of King Jesus and must invest in others as a disciple maker.

_____ TOTAL SCORE

If your TOTAL SCORE is:

40–50 You identify abiding time (Bible study, devotion, and prayer) as a source of strength in your life. Continue to develop new ways to study God's Word and communicate with him, and you will continue to see the benefit of your investment in the relationship.

30–39 You have the right idea but may lack consistent focus. Consider the ways your personal life, family, church, and community would benefit if you spent more time studying the Bible and talking with God plus listening to God.

20–29 You struggle with prioritizing time with God. Examine your daily schedule and habits to decide what changes you need to make to prioritize abiding time through Bible study and prayer.

SEEK THE HOLY SPIRIT

0–19   You clearly see the need for improvement in your study of God's Word and in your prayer and devotional life. Think about one person you could ask to help you develop these disciplines and keep you accountable. Be courageous! Keep growing.

Disciples grow. Jesus consistently used questions to encourage growth and invite people into discussion, and create invitations toward faith in him. In Acts 8, we see Philip, one of the seven appointed to tend to the needs of the church in Jerusalem (Acts 6:5–6), exemplify Jesus' discipleship process. The discipleship process always multiplies! Clearly the first apostles imitated Christ and made disciples. Philip was one of them.

READ the story in Acts 8:26–38.

ANSWER these questions:

1. How do you see Philip responding to the Holy Spirit in this passage?
2. Look specifically at the interactive questions between Philip and the eunuch. How does the Holy Spirit use questions as you intentionally disciple someone?
3. The passage from Isaiah 53:7–8 that the eunuch was reading gave Philip the opportunity to "[tell] him the good news about Jesus" (Acts 8:35). When has the

Holy Spirit led you to use the Word of God to share the gospel? Share the story.

4. How can this Bible story be used to encourage a deeper dependence on the Holy Spirit while being a disciple maker?

Philip was prompted by the Holy Spirit. He asked good questions, answered questions, and waited to be invited into sharing the truth of the gospel. There was noticeable fruit in Philip's life. His sensitivity to the promptings of the Holy Spirit for the purpose of pointing people to believe in Jesus was evident. Let it be so in us too, for Christ's glory alone!

PRACTICE growing in love. Start off by reading 1 John 4:7–12.

To seek the Holy Spirit is to walk in the way of love, as Jesus modeled. As we abide in Christ, pray and fast, are patient with people, and focus on truth, love is the motive. Love for Jesus and for others is why we seek the Holy Spirit and cooperate with what he is doing.

1. Practice asking God to fill you with his love for those he desires for you to reach. Make this a practice and a priority. "We love because he first loved us" (1 John 4:19). Take a simple tally of how often you are acting or speaking out of a genuine loving motive toward others this week.

2. With love as the motive, practice pausing and asking the Holy Spirit to reveal where the heavenly Father is working so you can cooperate with his work. Even Jesus only did what he saw the Father doing (John 5:19). The purposeful pause—stopping and inquiring of the Holy Spirit—before speaking or doing takes practice. Again, keep a record of how many times you pause and inquire of the Holy Spirit before acting or speaking.

Note: While you are cooperating with God, keeping track of these intentional steps, remember that the goal is greater love, new awareness, more sensitivity, and close dependence on the Holy Spirit. The tally marks are not to keep score or rate yourself.

PRAY that the Holy Spirit will reveal himself to you personally as you intentionally seek his heart of love and his help as a disciple. Invite him to reveal where the Father is working as you look and listen for his promptings while growing as a disciple maker. Rejoice that the Holy Spirit will always guide you in ways that align with the Bible's truth and magnify Jesus.

SHELLY, A DISCIPLE MAKER

Seeking the Holy Spirit and *seeing* go hand in hand for me. Cooperating with the Spirit is vital to my faith walk and to making disciples. For me it involves prayer, spiritual sight, purposeful pause, then pursuit. God himself is a purposeful pursuer. If Jesus did nothing of his own accord but did only what he saw the Father doing (John 5:19), I want to do the same.

I must have planned time abiding in Christ to cooperate with the Holy Spirit to see with Jesus' loving eyes. I need time in God's Word, prayer that includes listening, plus trusted relationships with people who have my permission to speak needed correction and coaching. I am only effective as a disciple maker when fully dependent on God, with Christ's motive of love. I consciously practice Paul's instructions to "pray without ceasing" (1 Thess. 5:17 ESV). I am purposefully pausing and prayerfully asking, "God, who do you see? Where are you working?" Jesus does prompt me to *see* who needs his unconditional, matchless love. The Holy Spirit highlights people, giving prompts or short phrases of instruction.

One day I was walking my dog in our neighborhood. I saw a family dressed all in black who stepped out of a dark limo. I did not know them, but the Lord let me *see* them. From a distance, I saw only the build of their bodies and hair color, yet the Holy

Spirit imprinted them on my mind. I paused, inquired of the Lord, then felt prompted by the Spirit to pray for them as I kept walking, knowing that grief was most likely what they were experiencing. For several days, every time I drove or walked by their home, the Holy Spirit prompted me to pray for them. He was building a love for them in my heart, even though I had never met them. The ways of God are beautiful.

Prayer always leads me to action, and I wanted to meet the lady of the home. In my spirit, I felt that I *must*. The "pause" was over, and it was time to act in obedience. I bought a sympathy card, wrote a simple note inside, and left the card along with my address and phone number on their front porch. What is usually my verbal introduction was now handwritten: "Hi! My name is Shelly, your neighbor. I saw your family the day that you probably attended a funeral. I'm genuinely sorry you are hurting. The Lord is prompting me to pray for you. I'd also really like to meet you and get to know you." A few days later, the lady of the home stopped by as I was outside, introduced herself, and agreed to a coffee date. The Holy Spirit was working. I was cooperating. I knew it. So I kept praying, with thankfulness and expectation for what God would do.

Sitting across a table from a woman sharing her story is an absolute favorite space of mine! Being an intentional disciple maker requires proximity and time. I listen a lot and talk very little at first. While listening, I am silently praying and asking the Holy Spirit to help me hear what I need to pay attention to. I am also watching for what *lights up* her face. I can often tell what is tender or even painful by noticing changes in her countenance or body language. *Seeing* someone is practical awareness, with humble reliance on the Holy Spirit.

Because seeing needs remembering, after our conversation is over, I write notes to myself of specifics the Holy Spirit has revealed. Writing down names, special dates, or significant pieces of a woman's story helps me pray specifically for her plus live intentionally as a disciple maker. I use these notes for prayer and for refreshing my memory before meeting again. I want to love women well. Small remembrances matter a lot.

As a relationship grows, I keep pausing to inquire of the Holy Spirit. I trust God for when to share the gospel and the imperative responses toward Christ's good news. As a woman submits to Jesus' lordship, I continue being a Spirit-led disciple maker. I make weekly appointments to meet with her and share my life in Christ with her. I don't just talk about having a "quiet time." I come alongside her so she can see the habits that keep me passionate about knowing Christ and the wonders of his person through the Bible. I ask questions, give appropriate challenges, and offer much encouragement. As spiritual growth happens, the time between our meetings together lengthens but connection continues. Nothing is sweeter than seeing a woman hunger for more of God and starting her own deliberate pursuit so that she can see Christ and herself *in him* rightly.

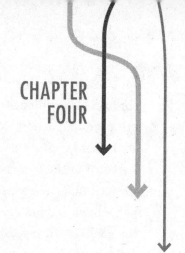

CHAPTER
FOUR

DEVELOP POTENTIAL

Over the stadium intercom, the track meet announcer called out my name. "Brandon Guindon—1992 Idaho State Champion for shot put." I could see my parents waving and clapping from the stands of Boise State University. Though I was only a high school kid, I had already accomplished one of my dreams— winning the state championship. As I stood on the podium awaiting my medal, my heart flooded with pride for all the hard work I had done, but there was also a deep appreciation and gratitude for all my coach had invested in me. Four years prior to that gold medal hanging around my neck, a coach had seen something in me that I did not. My coach believed I had potential. And he invested in my life in such a way that he was able to draw out that potential.

I was always big for my age, but winning a state shot put championship takes more than just size. Coach Dan Nipp saw

55

my size and the raw athletic ability I had, but he also knew that through his molding and shaping there was a giftedness, a work ethic, and a passion that could be tapped to form me into a state champion. He saw my potential, and for hours every day I trained in the gym as he relentlessly pushed me to improve my technique. Long after most other kids went home, I stayed at the track and practiced. My coach pushed me to accomplish my goals and never let up, developing something in me that I did not and could not see myself. For four years he pushed, challenged, and even, at times, demanded effort from me that left to myself, I would not have pursued.

Becoming an intentional disciple maker—a disciple who makes a disciple—is an intricate and ongoing process of spiritual development. When disciple making becomes an unconscious-capable skill, we will live it out without thinking about what we are doing. As Jesus developed this potential in his disciples, he did it because it was a natural part of who he was. And that's something we need to remember. Developing our potential is what God does—it's part of who God is. He desires us to become who he fully created us to be, and God gave each person gifts and abilities to live out this calling in the body of Christ. When we, in turn, develop that potential in others, we are not working alone or against God's purposes. We are simply being obedient to what God empowers us to do. Ultimately, God is the one who develops any potential we might possess. He's the one who put that potential there in the first place!

Jesus began building his church by developing a group of ragtag fishermen. He could have stood on the temple steps and lectured for hours upon hours. He could have limited his ministry to weeklong evangelistic crusades that called tens of thousands to repentance. Yet that is not what he did. Jesus' primary focus was to develop the twelve men he called to be his disciples. By investing relationally in those closest to him, he developed their potential as leaders, pastors, and great "fishers of men." These fishermen followed the guidance of the Holy Spirit and ignited the mission of Christ, transforming the world. The "least likely" turned into some of the most influential men in human history, largely because of Jesus' intentional investment in them as those called to follow him.

When I entered high school, I had no idea that one day I would stand atop a podium with a gold medal around my neck. And there is no way those fishermen thought they would one day lead the greatest movement ever to happen on planet Earth. My shot put career can hardly compare to the greatness of the apostles, but I will draw from it here some general principles about how people develop that we can apply in our disciple-making journeys.

Developing potential in others, combined with our first two practices, *listen to understand* and *seek the Holy Spirit*, are the core practices that form a lifestyle of disciple making. Here is where the rubber starts to meet the road. We begin to develop potential in others due to a growing sensitivity to the Holy Spirit's work, and we listen better to those in whom we invest. We start to see who and what someone else could become in Christ. We begin to see things others do not see in themselves, not because we are special but because we are hearing it from their own lips. As we listen, waiting on God, he often points out to us things that people cannot see for themselves, things that we might even miss if we aren't listening to God.

Nothing in my twenty-plus years of ministry has been more gratifying than learning to recognize untapped potential in people and then investing in them so that raw material comes alive. When we develop potential in others, we release the created purpose God has intended for them. We partner with the Holy Spirit and help others become who God designed them to be for the advancement of the kingdom.

Tom joined my small group, and for the first two months, he hardly said a word. He came to our group at the invitation of another group member, Ron. The two men worked together, and Tom, a younger unmarried man, was going through a very difficult time. Eventually, as he attended several weeks, Tom began to open up, and I knew I wanted to get to know him better. Tom loved golf, and one morning after our small group met, he invited me to play golf with him. There was only one problem: I am not a golfer and do not enjoy the game. While golf is a rather relaxed sport, at the end of a day of golf, I find myself far from relaxed. (It may be that I'm just too stinking competitive!)

Nevertheless, I jumped at the opportunity to spend several hours riding in a golf cart with Tom. By the third hole, I had learned a tremendous amount as I listened to understand Tom. His story was painful to hear, filled with abuse and betrayal. By the ninth hole, I could see that Tom loved Jesus but felt he had little to no worth. He genuinely believed God could never use him. At thirty-one years old, with a whole life ahead of him, Tom believed he was outside of God's power, love, and grace, and he had a difficult time seeing how God could use him in any significant way.

By the time we reached the thirteenth hole, however, Tom

had begun to dream. He trusted me enough to share some glimmers of hope he had for the future. He had passions to be tapped hidden deep in his soul, and in particular Tom wanted to help teenagers and share the gospel with them. When I asked him some questions, Tom shared the gospel of Jesus Christ with ease. He beautifully communicated truth, and excitement poured out of him as he shared his own testimony. I could see that Tom needed someone to invest in him, to develop his potential.

We pulled up to the eighteenth hole, and by that time we had caught up to the group in front of us. As we sat in the cart waiting, I asked Tom a question. "Tom, what if you and I started to meet one-on-one and I discipled you?" He looked back in shock. I continued, "You and I could meet outside of group for an additional hour or so and see where God takes it. I am going to push you and challenge you in several areas of your life. Would you want that?" Tears formed in Tom's eyes. He looked away, and fidgeting with his golfing glove, he said, "Man, I would love that."

PRINCIPLES OF THE PRACTICE

Throwing a twelve-pound metal ball in high school with any kind of success is about more than picking it up and tossing it. It requires mastering many individual movements, learning one step or position at a time, and then practicing how those all fit together in a fluid motion. For hours, I watched film and performed repetitious drills to improve the craft of shot putting. And over years of making disciples, I've come to see that developing potential in others can similarly be broken down into several smaller, critical components. Developing the potential I saw in Tom started with some basic principles. In this section, we'll look at five key principles to help you recognize, practice, and implement as you seek to develop potential in someone you are discipling. As we look at each one, attempt to identify how it can be applied in your everyday life.

See What God Sees

When my high school coach first watched me throw a shot, I am sure he saw more mistakes in my form than he could count. However, he looked past the flaws and saw the potential instead. Similarly, when we first begin discipling someone, we, too, must look past the flaws. Thankfully, we all know what this is like because God does the same thing with all of us. When we surrender our lives to Christ and follow Jesus as a disciple, we're a mess of selfishness, sin, and bad habits. Then the Holy Spirit begins forming us into the likeness of Christ, a process that takes a lifetime. But through it all, God looks at us and sees the potential of what is to come. He sees the image of his Son being formed in us.

I have met countless people like my friend Tom. They join my small group or come through the doors of the church on Sunday, but few actually live up to the potential within them. Their experiences with church rarely involve someone investing in them, challenging them to volunteer and serve, or taking the time to disciple them. This is what we're trying to change! And to change, we must adjust our vision to see what God sees. When you meet someone new, don't be thrown off by what appears on the surface. Try looking deeper, asking God to help you see the potential he has placed inside that person.

One of the guys on my staff, who happens to be a close friend, is the perfect example of seeing what God sees lived out. Rob is bald, covered in tattoos, and dressed as though he came straight off the streets of Houston—like the leader of a tough street gang. When I first met Rob, he came into our church with a strong "stay back and do not talk to me" look. He was distant and quiet. I didn't need to ask if Rob had a tough life, and my curiosity drove me to get to know him. After Rob had attended our Sunday services for a couple of weeks, I pushed through his rough exterior and asked if we could meet. He agreed.

One evening Rob and I met at the church. He came through the doors, full-on gangster walk and dressed for the part. When we sat down, Rob began to share a bit about his past but focused more on how God had transformed him. He focused even more on all the ministry he had done in the last few years. He began to list all the things he had done, and I knew in that moment Rob wanted me to approve of him. I wondered if under this rough exterior was a guy just looking for someone to accept him. While he spoke, I intentionally listened to understand him and silently prayed for God to reveal to me what he wanted for Rob. History and a sense from God told me just to love Rob right where he was. Our meeting ended, and I knew I wanted Rob to get involved somewhere in the church. From what he had told me about his background, I saw his potential for one day becoming a powerful leader in our recovery ministry.

Over the next few months, Rob and his wife, Joni, got more involved in our church. They joined a small group and started to serve in some ministries. Slowly Rob was given more responsibilities, and our relationship grew. I saw gifts and potential in Rob because, along with other members of our ministry team,

I was looking for them. I did not try to put Rob in a mold or have him serve in a role that did not fit him. I looked for Rob's potential and sought God on how Rob could serve in our body. By seeing what God saw, I was able to identify Rob's gifts.

Identify Individual Gifts

Gift assessments can be found in abundance. We even use one in our church. But no gift assessment can replace what you learn from being in relationship—looking for what God is doing in someone's life and then identifying the gifts that person has. Assessments are helpful, but to develop someone's potential, a disciple maker must actually see the gifts God has given lived out in that person.

We recognize gifts when we spend time with others. There is no other way. Imagine trying to coach someone to do something but never being near them. In my shot put days, my coach would stand close to me, watching my every move, adjusting my foot placement or talking me through a change in body position. We must be in close relationship with those we are discipling, walking together, to truly see the gifts they possess.

When I first met Rob, I did not see the remarkable gift he has to draw someone into conversation and challenge them to grow. Rob has this God-given ability to have hard conversations with people while making them feel truly loved. Once I had a better relationship with Rob, I saw this gift in him all the time. His strength for working with difficult people comes not only from his past experiences but is also a gift given by the Holy Spirit. God helped me identify this gift in Rob, and I gave him the encouragement and opportunity to use it. God gave him the skills, and I gave him a place to play.

Give Places to Play

Rob eventually began to lead a men's group in our recovery ministry. Some of the most difficult, wounded, and hurting men in our church flooded to Rob's small group. Over the course of a year, I watched God use Rob to radically impact the lives of others. Rob's gifts were on full display, and he thrived in that environment. The kingdom advanced not only in our church but also in the lives of individuals. Rob was now "in the game" and growing as a disciple of Jesus.

For a moment, let's return to that first meeting I had with Rob at the church. In that conversation, Rob tried to prove to me that he should be welcomed into our church because of his past work. In my mind, Rob was already welcome in our church because of Christ, not because of his resumé. I wanted Rob to experience something deeper than the list of his past accomplishments. I wanted him to encounter unconditional love and to discover opportunities to get in the game in our church and be part of our team. As I listened, I noticed that in every case where Rob described his ministry, he was alone. He ministered to hurting people—but all on his own. I wanted Rob to see that he didn't have to go it alone. I wanted him to feel the love and acceptance of our church for who he was and not just for what he did.

Rob grew so much in his first year at our church that we started to see a call to full-time vocational ministry in his life. I had observed Rob working with others and trusting the leadership of our church. He shifted from being guarded and closed down to being one of the strongest disciple makers in our entire church. His gifts were being used, and with a place to play, Rob flourished in the body of Christ.

Embrace Mistakes

When we develop potential in others, mistakes *are* going to happen. I have heard it said that church would be so much easier if people were not involved. Sometimes I tend to agree. Even some of Jesus' responses to people who lacked faith had that feel to them. Intentional disciple making is not for the faint of heart. So when a mistake is made, be ready to embrace the person who made it and to work through the fallout together.

Earlier I shared about my daughter and her rehabilitation from brain injury. If you remember, she lived through a process of relearning skills and habits and moving from unconscious incapable to unconscious capable. This did not happen quickly or easily. Her days were filled with hundreds if not thousands of mistakes. She spent countless hours just learning to tie her shoes. She made mistake after mistake until she could finally perform the task on her own. Today she can tie her shoes without a conscious thought—but it took intentional work and effort to get to that place.

Just like Olivia, Rob made all kinds of mistakes. After two full years of Rob volunteering and leading in our church, we offered him an opportunity to join the church staff full-time. Rob stepped into that role as an associate pastor and began leading our recovery ministry. Within just a few short weeks, however, Rob experienced a major conflict with one of the volunteers on his team.

When the conflict arose, we scheduled a meeting so we could work it out together. I will never forget how nervous Rob was. I knew we were going to get the conflict resolved, but Rob believed it could end his job. We all sat down, and I listened to the volunteer share how Rob had offended him. Rob did an excellent job of listening to understand; he did not defend himself, and he listened well. I sat back and watched in amazement as the Holy Spirit restored a broken relationship.

Did Rob make a mistake in what he said to the volunteer and how he initially handled the incident? Yes. But what can we take away from Rob's story? We will all make mistakes and must learn to embrace them and turn them into opportunities instead. In helping someone grow, we take another step forward in developing the person's potential. Rob learned multiple lessons from this one event, but most of all he learned that everyone makes mistakes and that we can work through anything together. The mistake became a win.

Affirm Progress

When I affirm someone for the development I see in them, it motivates them further and provides fuel to continue the journey. Walking through the conflict with Rob and our volunteer was hard, but Rob learned from that experience, and the next time he had a conflict with a volunteer, he knew how to handle it well. Over time he has even helped others navigate difficult situations. I need to make the effort to tell Rob that I appreciate the progress I've seen him make in regard to resolving conflict. Affirming him along the way cements the hard work and sacrifice he has made. It marks what was accomplished as good and reinforces that what has been developed in him is worth celebrating. God is glorified and intentional disciple making advances.

Each one of us is surrounded by people who have no idea what God could do through them. Tom went on to be one of the most outstanding volunteer leaders I've seen in youth ministry.

He led students to Christ and discipled many. Rob continues to serve as an associate pastor, ministering to those broken by addiction and pain.

Both Tom and Rob have impacted the kingdom of God because someone saw their potential and cultivated it. Just think of what might happen if each of us were to take the time to do the same for someone else. Jesus went to some guys throwing nets in the sea. He called them, and they responded, not knowing what God would do in them and through them. Their simple willingness to follow Jesus in disciple making eventually led to a global church of countless people over two thousand years. This book is a by-product of that investment made two millennia ago. And more recently I am forever grateful to the people in my life who saw my own potential, whether it was my high school coach Dan Nipp, or my dear friend Jim Putman at Real Life Ministries. They invested in my life and developed the potential God placed in me that in turn has been used to invest in many others. So open your eyes, look for potential in others, and then develop it. God will take care of the results.

Experience and Apply

When we seek God, he will give direction or illuminate the potential in others. Intentional disciple makers look for the potential in others.

List the five practices of developing potential. After each practice, rate your current level of proficiency with that practice. Use a scale from 1 to 5 where 1 = not intentional at all, and 5 = very intentional.

1. _____. ____
2. _____. ____
3. _____. ____
4. _____. ____
5. _____. ____

The five practices you should have listed are: (1) see what God sees; (2) identify individual gifts; (3) give places to play; (4) embrace mistakes; and (5) affirm progress.

List people in your life who have identified and developed potential in you, such as a parent, teacher, or coach. Reflect on the ways in which they did this.

_____
_____
_____
_____
_____

Paul spent many years persecuting Christians, but when he encountered Jesus personally, he was changed. His life became a mission to spread the gospel as far as he was able. At the beginning of his second missionary journey, he met a young man named Timothy. Let's read more about the relationship between Paul and Timothy.

READ Acts 16:1–5. Now read what Paul wrote to the churches about Timothy in Philippians 2:19–24. Finally, read Paul's words to Timothy many years later in 2 Timothy 3:10–17.

ANSWER these questions:

1. What was it about Paul and Timothy's relationship that made Paul's message powerful to Timothy?
2. What might keep you from engaging in these types of relationships?
3. It has been said that everyone needs a Paul and a Timothy. Who is your Paul? (Who is developing potential in you and speaking into your life?) Who is your Timothy? (Who are you discipling, developing, and investing in?)
4. Paul intentionally invested in Timothy. What impact did this have on the early church?

PRACTICE developing potential by identifying a gift or ability you see in someone else (e.g., child, coworker, or friend) and speak that into their life. Share with someone else (e.g., spouse or small group) how that conversation went.

PRAY that God helps you to see gifts in yourself and in someone else. Ask God if you need to find someone to help develop you. Ask him how you can begin to develop someone else.

GREG, A DISCIPLE MAKER

Nine months after our family moved to Texas, Hurricane Harvey hit the area and our home was one of many that was flooded. We did not have any flood insurance, nor did we have any family or friends close by who could help us clean up after the rain stopped. A group of volunteers from a nearby church showed up at my door and asked if we needed any help cleaning up. We had not belonged to a church for a long time and were still dealing with church hurt. My wife and I were both standing at the door, and she said to me, "Swallow your pride and accept the help," so that is what I did. As much as I didn't want to make conversation, one of the guys insisted on asking us question after question after question.

A week after the cleanup was done, I received a phone call from the guy who asked endless questions. He invited me to join him and several other guys just to hang out. Similar to the week before, everything in me wanted to say no. Looking back, I know God was at work. Again, my wife encouraged me to go, and that is where my friendship with the guy who called and other men at the church began.

Over the next few months, I visited with that guy regularly. Several times he invited me to join him and several others to sit on his patio talking together. God was drawing me closer, and all I knew was that something was happening, and my life seemed to be changing. Then one day these guys invited me to a men's breakfast at the church. I justified going because, technically, it wasn't *church*.

They really hooked me into coming, because in one of our conversations I had shared that I loved to cook. When they said to me, "By the way, we also need you to cook the breakfast for us," I knew I had to go. Culinary arts is a passion of mine, and the guys I had been hanging out with knew that. When I arrived at the church to cook breakfast and saw what I had to work with, I wanted to get back in my truck and go home! I saw a twenty-four-inch griddle that belonged in a museum, plastic spatulas and tongs, and pancake mix with directions to just add water and shake. There were about twenty men and maybe five middle-school-aged boys standing around.

I went over to the boys and asked if they wanted to give me a hand. Hesitantly they agreed, and we started making breakfast. I instructed them to prep the eggs and pancake mix, but it was clear that these boys had no clue what they were doing. I found eggshells in the bowl with the eggs and pancake batter all over the prep area, griddle, and the boys themselves. I started showing them how to do the prep and asked them questions along the way. Two of the boys, Grady and Garret, seemed more interested in learning than the others, so I spent more time with them, explaining breakfast prep in greater detail. From then on, I led the cooking team at our monthly men's breakfast. As the months went by, Grady and Garret became my right-hand helpers. They were soon able to prep and cook without me looking over their shoulders.

A few months later, I was asked to participate in the

training the church holds for their leaders twice each year. I did not see myself as a leader in the church, so I questioned why I should attend, but I went because I was invited. During the training, my facilitator pointed out to me that unconsciously I was discipling these boys and developing a talent in them. I had never even thought of it in that way.

Grady and Garret are going to be seniors in high school this year, and this summer Garret worked as a line cook in a restaurant. I now watch as Grady and Garret walk alongside other boys in the youth ministry, teaching them how to cook for the monthly men's breakfast the same way I did with them.

TAKE SOMEONE WITH YOU

Each year I invite several staff, elders, and volunteers from our church to join me in attending various conferences. One particular conference focused on church planting and other aspects of Christian leadership, and at this conference I had the opportunity to speak on building a disciple-making culture in the local church. Events like these provide a great opportunity for me to invest in people from our church and build relationships. Along with that, I can expose others from our church to the greater mission of Jesus' call to go make disciples. They get a sense of the impact we have as a church and the role they play in our own church as we live out disciple making at home.

One year, as we walked to our gate at the airport, I was with my friends James and Denise. James is a strong, charismatic leader who loves people like few I have ever seen, and Denise is a kind, gentle woman, very intentional in discipling younger women in one-on-one settings. At the time, they were serving as volunteers in our youth ministry, and God was moving powerfully in their lives. Anyone in our church who knew them saw the tremendous influence they were having on both youth and other adult volunteers. So, when the opportunity came to take them with me to this conference, I jumped at it. And even though the call to ministry stood out in their lives, walking through the airport that day, I could tell that they did not see this for themselves. Little did they know that God had something great in store for them.

Pulling her suitcase through the terminal, Denise walked close to my side and said, "Brandon, I have no idea why I am here. I understand inviting James, but what is the point in me coming along?"

I paused for a moment. "Well, Denise, I invited you because I see God doing great things in you and James. I have no idea what all God has planned for you, but I know my part in obedience is inviting you to come along. I feel that it is also my role to challenge you to grow and to put both of you in circumstances for God to help you see what he sees in you."

"So, this conference does all of that?" she asked.

I smiled at her, knowing God was going to move in a mighty way. I've seen many people in similar circumstances, and I believed Denise and James would be no different in responding to God's call.

"No, it's not the conference," I replied. "Sure, the conference is good, but it's the discussions we have after the content is shared that are really valuable. We spend time together having conversations that are vital in processing what God might be saying to you. Frankly, I'm not sure what God will show you, but I do know that he always does his part. I also know that I must invite you along for the ride."

"That is terrifying," Denise responded.

I smiled again and said, "Well, following Jesus can be a terrifying thing. We will see how God leads, but if nothing else, we can have a great time together, and our group will build stronger relationships."

One of the most powerful foundational principles of the Christian faith is that we no longer need to do life alone. Christ's sacrifice made a way for relationship with him and with one another. Not only are we supposed to be in relationship, but we also belong to one another (John 13:35). Relationship is not an optional luxury reserved for those who are socially outgoing. Blessing, support, and encouragement are found in Christian fellowship. Unfortunately, in many churches we have neglected to implement Jesus' model of sending people out two by two. We have underestimated the power of relationship when learning to do ministry together. When this happens, the church suffers from not recognizing the power of a key ingredient of the Christian life—fellowship.

Naturally, when we become more intentional in our own spiritual growth, we invite others along with us. Relationship is a necessity because we are called to do life together. Christ's sacrifice and resurrection opened a door that sets disciples of Jesus apart. We live in a spiritual community, and the process of disciple making was always intended to happen in this holy community. Real, intentional disciple making happens in the context of being together with other believers, following Christ together. Removing or distancing ourselves from one another injects a dysfunctional disease that can rot the community Jesus has established. We must not allow that to happen.

I love these words of Dietrich Bonhoeffer in his short book on Christian community: "What determines our brotherhood is what that man is by reason of Christ. Our community with one another consists solely in what Christ has done to both of us."[2] When I invited James and Denise to go along with me to the conference, it was not to build up my ego or because I needed support for one of my speaking events. Quite the opposite. I invited them because I knew what God could do for them. It was about their development, about us walking together and being obedient to Christ's call to serve him in this way. They needed the opportunity to see and experience what broader ministry looks like. This invitation was about doing my part, knowing God would do his, and praying that James and Denise would do theirs.

Today's church fails to engage in intentional disciple making for many reasons. But a core reason is our cultural habit of distancing ourselves from one another. In this, we tragically follow how much of the rest of the world engages in relationship. Herein lies the problem. We attend Sunday morning services in masses, and even lift our voices in unified song, but rarely do we have relationships where we know others and are known by them. Real life relationships are the glue that holds intentional disciple making together, and without these relationships, the whole idea of relational discipleship becomes just another program.

Jesus modeled something much different for us. He said that the greatest commandment is to love God, and the second is like it, to love one another (Matt. 22:36–40). These are commandments, not suggestions. When relationships become central for us, we become more unconscious capable in our disciple making. And we look more like what Jesus modeled when we recognize the power of *taking someone along.*

Whether he was feeding a crowd of thousands, teaching a handful of people about God's love, or healing an individual, Jesus kept his disciples right by his side. He took them with him everywhere because he knew that for them to imitate his life, they had to see what it looked like up close and personal.

We, too, must follow in Jesus' steps and embrace his model as the master disciple maker. Practically this means intentionally inviting others to "go along" with us as we do life. When I asked James and Denise to join our group traveling to the conference, I was participating in the process Jesus modeled. This made a way for further growth to occur. I knew that James and Denise would benefit not only from the conference but also from the dozens of conversations about what God was doing in their lives.

PRINCIPLE OF THE PRACTICE

As I reflect on my own life of disciple making and look at the life of Christ, I can identify five key principles that highlight the importance of taking others along as we go. Let's dive into what it means to provide a model, grow in relationship, enjoy shared experiences, ask good questions, and finally, impart your knowledge.

Provide a Model

I stood next to my friend and former pastor Jim Putman, and I could tell by the look on his face that the call he had received was not good. His face turned pale, and he looked at me with desperation. He hung up the phone and said, "We've got to go." I followed him out the door of our offices and into his truck, having no idea what was going on. While pulling out of the driveway, he said, "This isn't going to be good." Jim explained to me that a family in our church had just suffered an accident at home. With few details from the father, the best Jim could tell was that their sixteen-year-old child had been killed in the accident.

At that time, I had just three months of full-time ministry under my belt. I had yet to experience the kind of tragedy that leads to this type of phone call. While making our way to the hospital, Jim made several other phone calls, asking people to pray. As he finished up his last phone call, we pulled into the hospital emergency parking lot. I will never forget what happened next.

The doors of the emergency room burst open. A woman came out screaming and wailing in agony. Then she collapsed on the sidewalk in front of the emergency room doors. Jim looked at me and said, "That's the mom." The dad came out of the emergency room crying, and all of us together helped the mom to her feet. As Jim and I stood there comforting this couple, we did not need to hear the words; we knew they had lost their child. In that moment and in the days to come, I watched closely as Jim ministered to this family. I had no idea what to do in a terrible crisis like this. Jim kept me at his side every step of the way, even through the funeral and following up with the family. He provided a model for me, showing me what it looked like to care for a hurting family. He modeled something I had no idea how to do, and during that tragedy and in the days that followed, I learned what it meant to sit with a devastated family in their loss. I watched Jim deliver the funeral message and witnessed a church organizing meals to care for someone in need.

I tell this story not because I think everyone should be in full-time ministry, learn to preside at a funeral, or even know how to minister to someone in the emergency room. This was an extreme event, and I share it simply as an example of what it means to invite someone alongside you. Jim invited me to come alongside him because he knew the importance of living out what disciple making truly is by modeling it in front of me. I had no idea what to do in that situation, but now I do. Because Jim intentionally took me with him, I learned.

And because of Jim's example, I also learned the value of inviting others to go along with me. Whether I'm visiting someone at the hospital or sharing the gospel with a nonbeliever, I commonly bring someone with me so that I model what it looks like to minister in both the good and the bad. Jesus did this for his disciples, and we must do the same to pass on the fundamentals of intentional disciple making.

One reason the book of Acts exists in our Bibles is because Jesus first invited his disciples to follow him. They were given a model to minister to hurting people, to care for those in need, and even to recognize opportunities to preach the gospel. The very layout of the New Testament letters follows the life of Christ because Jesus invited his disciples to walk alongside him. He provided them with the model.

Grow in Relationship

When we invite someone to go along with us, the critical elements of proximity and time come into play. The very word *together* implies the idea of spending time close to one another. When I invited James and Denise to the conference with me, we were in close proximity for an entire week and had countless hours of discussion. In these moments together, we got to know one another far better than when we began the trip. We shared stories and grew deeper in relationship. Our time together was valuable, and thinking of that I can only imagine the countless conversations the disciples had with Jesus as they walked along the road or sat around a table sharing a meal together. I am confident that in each conversation, Jesus was modeling for his disciples how they should live in obedience to God and they were growing through it all.

Inviting people to come along with us means we're inviting them into deeper relationship. This is a benefit both parties gain. Together we experience what God is doing in each other's lives, and we grow in the process.

When I think about strong relationships built because I took someone along with me, I immediately think of Greg, a close friend who works on staff at our church in the area of missions and church planting. He and I have traveled all over the world together, teaching leaders and churches about intentional disciple making. I often invite Greg to come along with me, not only because he's my friend and part of our staff, but because it is during these times that we grow in relationship as we share in the work of ministry together. On these trips, we discuss Scripture and talk about how God's truth applies to life. God has prompted me to speak into Greg's life on multiple occasions, and he has spoken into my life as well. Not only do we process the truth of Scripture, but we also grow in our relationship as brothers in Christ. Taking someone with me where I go opens doors to these kinds of deeper relationships.

Enjoy Shared Experiences

I love road trips—and perhaps that is one reason why I love bringing people along with me wherever I go. And although Jesus didn't travel by bus or plane, when we examine his life, we see that he and his disciples were on what looks like a perpetual road trip. They moved from place to place, experiencing the good and the bad together, and I believe that was intentional. One day Jesus told his disciples that he would soon leave them and the Holy Spirit would come. At the time, they didn't fully understand what that meant, but as the days passed and Jesus ascended to heaven after his death and resurrection, the Holy Spirit did come and the church was born. And as the church grew, the disciples remembered their shared experiences with Jesus and were encouraged and strengthened for the tasks ahead. They had a reference point for what it looked like to care for a crowd or to minister to the hurting. They had three years of watching Jesus model the very actions they now needed to emulate.

Taking people with us creates shared experiences. And every experience is an opportunity for us to look at one another and say, "Remember when . . . ?" We remember the times of learning, times of hardship, and definitely the times of celebration, and the remembering is beautiful.

In your own life, I am sure you can reflect on times when God moved in your life and you were able to share that moment with someone. Maybe it was serving on a mission trip, leading someone to Christ, or simply praying with a hurting friend. When you intentionally take someone along on life's journey, life becomes filled with shared experiences. You find that you never have to say, "You just had to be there."

Ask Good Questions

One evening I got a phone call and learned that someone in my small group had suddenly become ill and had been admitted to the hospital. As soon as I finished the call, I jumped at the opportunity to take someone with me and called my small group apprentice, Brian, because he knew the family. I picked him up, and we went to the hospital together. On the way, Brian asked me questions about what to expect as this would be his first trip to a hospital to minister to someone in need.

By the time we arrived, the doctors had determined that our small group member's issue was just a severe case of food poisoning—not life-threatening. We prayed with the family and left, and while driving home I had the opportunity to discuss the experience with Brian. I asked him what he had seen me do and what he had learned. Brian described things like praying with the family, staying for only a short time, and letting them know that we had arranged meals to care for their other family members. He saw that even though we were there for only a short time, we were still able to care for the family and show them God's love.

Some other great questions you can ask when you take someone with you are:

- What was our part in this? What was God's part? What was the other person's part?
- What did you see the Lord do?

- What did you learn about yourself?
- What was a fear you had going into the experience? How did that play out?
- How will you respond next time you have an opportunity like this?

As we got closer to home, I encouraged Brian, telling him that he could do what I did. I shared with him times in the past when I had learned from others. The car ride allowed me to ask him questions, and it allowed him to process what he had just experienced. I share this with you because Jesus did the exact same thing. Whether it was the twelve disciples, Mary and Martha, or the Jewish leaders, Jesus asked questions about what they had just seen or experienced. Don't assume anything. Hear disciples' hearts and listen to what they learned. Encourage, correct, and challenge them.

Impart Your Knowledge

The last component when taking someone with us is imparting our knowledge. And it's important that this is the final component. We started with the idea of a model, then moved to the relational components of growing in relationship, sharing experiences, and asking good questions. Now we intentionally impart knowledge, or in other words, we share the things we have learned. We do this last because it makes sense in the context of the other components. We will have earned the relational equity needed to impart our knowledge to those we have taken with us.

Why do I raise this topic? Because I'm concerned that disciple making in most of today's churches has become so focused on imparting knowledge that *we forget that knowledge is best passed on in the context of real-life relationships.* As disciple making becomes more and more something we do as unconscious capable, we think less about all the great facts we can teach and instead focus on life change for the other person. When we do share the knowledge we have learned from following Christ, we do so in a context of relationship that communicates integrity and authenticity.

Reflect on the things Jesus did and recall the story of him speaking with the Samaritan woman at the well. Jesus first spent relational time with her discussing her water-fetching habits and the mess that her life had become. Then, and only then, did he share truth with her. He imparted the powerful knowledge of who he was and what that could mean for her way of life. Similarly, Jesus often waited until after an event was over to impart knowledge to his disciples. We must resist the urge to rush in and tell someone all that we know on a topic. Instead, trust the process, the journey you are on with them. As life unfolds and you have built a relationship of trust, impart the knowledge God has given to you.

In the church, we seem to have missed a principle applied in many occupations. During their training, new surgeons follow, watch, observe, and then, under close observation, practice the skill of that discipline. Young athletes watch and learn from those who are further along and more talented. Student teachers observe and apprentice with more-experienced teachers before they take on their own classroom. The list goes on and on, yet sadly, in the church we somehow think that a person can be discipled by attending a weekly Sunday service or sitting in a classroom learning Bible facts.

Intentional disciple making requires close proximity. The lifestyle of a disciple demands intimate knowledge of spiritual practices that are best learned from a more seasoned disciple. When we take someone with us as we go, we are following the model Jesus exhibited. When we do as Jesus commands, we see lives changed. We see people experiencing what it means to be disciples who go and make disciples. After attending that conference with me, my friends James and Denise went on to plant a church, and now they, too, are taking others with them as they go and make disciples.

Experience and Apply

When do you have opportunities to take someone with you to model disciple making, grow in relationship together, enjoy shared experiences, ask good questions, and impart your knowledge?

You may have listed things such as going to the grocery store, going to the hospital to visit someone, or participating in a hobby. "As you go," take someone with you.

Let's explore a story where Jesus included his disciples. When Jesus fed the five thousand, he could have said the word and the people would have been fed. Instead, Jesus brought the disciples along in the process.

READ the story in John 6:1–13.

ANSWER these questions:

1. What does Philip's response reveal?
2. How was Jesus intentional in including the disciples?
3. What keeps you from including someone else in your daily tasks?
4. What shift in perspective or attitude would help you begin to live a lifestyle in which taking someone with you becomes second nature?

PRACTICE taking someone with you. As you think about upcoming opportunities you have this week, take someone with you. Try to model disciple making, growing in relationship, enjoying shared experiences, asking good questions, and imparting your knowledge. Share your "as you go" experience with someone else.

PRAY that the Lord would prompt you to include others in your daily activities. Ask him to remove any fear of risk or inconvenience that would keep you from bringing someone along. Pray that your conversations and time spent with others would glorify the Lord and build his kingdom.

Snapshots

Taking Someone with You

COLLIN, A DISCIPLE MAKER

After leaving a career as a detective with the Houston Police Department to work in real estate with my wife, I found myself hiding from the world at my home on twelve secluded acres. I had no desire to spend time with people other than my wife and kids. All of that began to change when I walked through the doors of a church committed to intentional disciple making. The Lord opened my eyes to understand my purpose as a Christian: to go and make disciples of Jesus who make more and more disciples. I was excited that my life and purpose were changing, but I did not instinctively know how to make disciples.

I joined a small group, and one of the guys in my group, Lance, started calling me and inviting me to spend time with him. Lance would invite me to go pick something up from the store with him or to eat lunch together. He would ask me to go help set up for an event at his company. He continued to invite me to come along as he went about his day.

At first I found this unusual. Though I enjoyed our time together, I could not understand why he was not just doing these things on his own. He could have finished his tasks much more efficiently if he had done them alone. I wondered what his ulterior motives were, for he was persistent. Through our friendship and his intentionality, I started to grow spiritually.

As Lance continued to disciple me for over a year, I began to practically understand discipleship because I was experiencing it. Lance is now one of my best friends. We have been through some great times and some very difficult times together.

After Lance modeled inviting me along with him and discipling intentionally, I started the reproducible process with people in my life. My wife and I began leading a small group, and Jeremy and his wife joined our group. The Lord made it clear that I needed to disciple Jeremy, so I began a friendship with him the same way Lance modeled for me. I invited Jeremy to come with me as I did daily tasks like shopping, going to breakfast and lunch, and serving others in need. I even invited him along as I met with others who needed counsel. This gave us time to grow in relationship as we both continued to grow spiritually. Jeremy was able to experience discipleship modeled in his own life and watch in real time as I discipled others. He asked me hundreds of practical questions about discipling others. Because he came alongside me, I was able to debrief with Jeremy and share knowledge the Lord had given me.

I knew the Lord was changing Jeremy before my eyes, and I could see what the Lord was putting on his heart since we had time with and proximity to each other. Jeremy felt the Lord's call on his heart, and he is now working in full-time ministry. The Lord is using him in a powerful way to shepherd families and change their futures. Jeremy now takes someone along with him, so the reproducible disciple-making process continues.

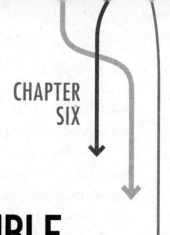

CHAPTER SIX

BE INTERRUPTIBLE

"Why now?" I grumbled as I got in my truck, started the ignition, and headed north.

I had just spent ten hours leading a conference at our church, and my emotional tank was running on empty. I also knew that the next morning I would be speaking at the same conference in front of several hundred people. All I wanted to do was go home and be alone for a little while to recharge and write down some notes about what I wanted to say. My topic was relational discipleship, and I needed some time to pray and put some new thoughts on paper.

A single phone call disrupted my plans for a quiet evening.

I could immediately tell the caller was panicked. "Brandon, this is Jen. Mike just called me. He shot a moose, but he's all by himself and has no way to get it off the mountain before the sun goes down. I'm scared, and I know he's alone. Would you please go help him? I don't even know where he is!"

Mike and Jen were a new couple in my small group, and Mike was an avid hunter. We had spent the previous few weeks talking about the special moose tag he had and how much he looked forward to the hunt. We discussed the area where he had decided to hunt and talked about his general plans. Jen was right, though. It was late fall, and Mike was alone with darkness setting in. Processing a thousand-pound animal was a massive job, but doing so alone in the dark was downright dangerous. Even with several men, it would have been a challenge.

On top of that, the potential of freezing temperatures that night could make the situation even more dangerous. There was no other option—I had to go get him. Mike was one of the first people I had ever led to the Lord. His wife had called me because she knew of my love for Christ, and she had learned, as I instructed her husband, that taking care of one another was part of the deal. So I abandoned the plan I had for myself at home that night and headed north. In addition, I called some of the men in our small group to help, all of whom also dropped their plans.

I knew the mountain where Mike was hunting. At its base, the public road ended and became a trailhead for ATVs. I parked my truck and began unloading my ATV, my mind racing, wondering where to even begin looking for Mike. Cell service was nonexistent, so I couldn't just call him and ask where he was. I was heartened to see that some of the men I called had already arrived at the site. We all loaded up, and I figured that Mike must be near a ridge top since he had been able to get a call out to Jen earlier in the day, telling her about the moose. So, myself and three other men headed out in the dark to find our friend.

Near the top of the mountain, we came around the bend and met up with another ATV. Thankfully, it was Mike! He beamed from ear to ear as he saw our familiar faces greeting him on the old trail. We turned off our vehicles, and he immediately recounted the story of shooting the moose and the challenge of getting it off the mountain. Collectively we all made lighter work of the cleaning, dressing, and packing of the thousand-pound moose and getting it to the bottom of the mountain. In the end, we were out there for several hours, and it was 3:30 a.m. before we got back home to load the moose into a large walk-in cooler. My heart sank as I remembered that I would be speaking at a conference in just a few hours. My plans for preparation were ruined, and in my mind I began to complain to God. But even as my complaints were forming, I looked over at Mike, and they stopped. Mike was in tears. This big, burly, manly moose hunter had tears running down his cheeks.

Startled, I asked him, "Mike, what's wrong?"

He was embarrassed but turned to me and said, "Now I understand what church is." The embarrassment instantly shifted to a look of joy.

Surprised by his answer, I asked, "What do you mean?"

"You guys were the church to me tonight," he said. "You sacrificed so much to come and help me. You were the church, and now I get it."

The next morning, with extra cups of coffee, I prepared to speak while navigating my brain fog from a lack of sleep. I said a little prayer, asking God to speak through me, because whatever I was going to say was going to have to come from him.

When looking down at the few notes I had, I will never forget what I heard whispered into my soul. The Holy Spirit spoke four simple words to me: "Just tell the story." As simple as that—just tell the story. So I shared the adventurous night before that I had with my friend, our small group, and the moose. As I shared what happened, I noticed a pastor in the front row crying. Not just a tear or two. He was crying like go-get-a-box-of-Kleenex, ugly crying. Others around him were in tears as well, but many kept a concerned eye focused on this pastor. I finally decided to stop speaking and ask him if he was okay. Everyone fixed their eyes on him.

This pastor, a man of God, with incredible bravery, stood up and looked over the room around him. With grief coating his confession, he said, "I pastor a church of fifteen hundred people, with a staff of twenty, and I don't have *anyone* I could ask to come help me pack a moose in the middle of the night."

With that one statement, God opened a door. Multiple church leaders in attendance admitted the same thing. These beautiful servants of the Lord had entered the ministry with no idea how to relationally disciple anyone—because they had never experienced it themselves. My story about helping a friend pack a moose awakened them to the void in their own lives and ministries. Now they were ready to hear anything else I had to say on the matter. Had I not experienced the craziness of the night before, I doubt that breakthrough would have come. Nothing I had prepared to say was as good as what God arranged for them to hear. God took my interruption and turned it into a holy moment that challenged church leaders to view disciple making in a whole new light.

When I think back on this occasion, I am still humbled by what God did that day. The impact of a simple story about a moose went far beyond what I could have thought up on my own. I had my own plan for how things were going to go, and God had his. God's plan was better. My mindset toward interruptions changed forever when I saw the outcome of that morning. I'm reminded of what Proverbs 19:21 says: "Many are the plans in a person's heart, but it is the LORD's purpose that prevails." Now I love watching God's plan win even when my own plans crash and burn.

If I have learned anything over the years, it is that disciple making is messy work. It's why I continue to say it's a lifestyle rather than a program. The more we invest in the lives of others, the more others will count on us. Some we disciple will take less time to mature spiritually as they become more others-focused. Many others, however, will require more of our time because in their spiritual infancy, they will have needs, questions, frustrations, and required maintenance that may not line up perfectly with our daily schedules. If we are going to be effective as disciple makers, we should expect interruptions. When these interruptions occur, we must be willing to stop what we are doing and serve them.

Since interruptions by their very nature are unplanned and oftentimes unwanted, it is hard to make a habit of having the right response to them. So, to be unconsciously capable in this area, we need to create more margin in our schedules. This will minimize the impact of interruptions and maximize our ability to serve well.

THE ADD AND SUBTRACT RULE

When interruptions happen, our natural response is to add them to our growing to-do lists for the day. The problem with this approach is that we end up adding more to do in a day but don't subtract anything. The interruption becomes just another thing to do. So here's the principle we need to embrace:

do not work longer hours to make up for time spent dealing with an interruption.

This may sound like an impossibility, but it is something we must learn to master with zero compromises. And here's why: If we allow the unscheduled opportunities to derail our plans so that we feel we must work longer, we will eventually miss out on things we want to do, like spending time with family, engaging in hobbies, or even resting. This will lead us to equate interruptions with loss and, in turn, resentment for the person we need to help. Those we disciple should not feel like their presence in our lives is an intrusion. We don't want them to build up walls that we will have to tear down later. The add and subtract rule of being interruptible means that when interruptions get added to our schedules, something must be subtracted as well.

I've heard it said that sometimes the most significant meetings are the ones we don't know we're going to have. We must learn to have this outlook in our disciple making. It means accepting the interruptions *as doing the Lord's work* and then finding something in our schedules that can be postponed in order to do the Lord's work. Admittedly this will require significant trust in God. Somehow our tasks will still get done and the world will stay in motion without us having to hold it up. Remember: interruptions are often unscheduled opportunities God gives us to serve him.

KEEP BANGING THE DRUM

As a church leader, I have found that many of my spontaneous meetings are precipitated by one of two things: someone wants to clarify something I said, or they want to better understand my expectations. In almost every case, these meetings happen because I tried to "save time" earlier and wasn't clear. I simply assumed that everyone understood what I meant, intended, or said and then neglected to follow up. How do I avoid more of these interruptions? I intentionally take time to overcommunicate with my family, staff, church members, and those I personally disciple. When I do this, I seem to find more time, enabling me to better handle the genuine interruptions God brings my way.

I call this practice of overcommunication "banging the drum." It's all about giving a consistent, clear message and then repeating it regularly until it's second nature. This is especially necessary when reminding others of our mission of making disciples. It's tempting for us, when we speak or communicate, to blindly keep moving ahead, assuming that since we've said it once, everyone is on board. But we know that we often forget or lose focus. We lose momentum. When we bang the drum on disciple making, we are realigning ourselves and others with the mission Jesus gave us.

Personally I do this by using videos, texts, emails, and messages from the pulpit to make sure no stone is left unturned for those I lead or disciple. I want to be clear, and I want people to remember what matters. And as I mentioned earlier, this practice of consistent communication actually helps eliminate many of the meetings or conversations that would likely happen if I was not as proactive.

To put it simply: spend extra time communicating and you'll have more time for other things. Banging the drum gives me an opportunity to lead intentionally by staying on message and managing the conversation. By investing in a little extra focus and time, it clears up much of the ambiguity and uneasiness others sometimes feel. Overcommunication isn't just for pastors and leaders, either. It works in marriages, parenting, and businesses, helping to create more margin in the schedule so you can deal with necessary interruptions while limiting unnecessary disturbances.

Learn to bang the drum. In discipling someone, call them, send messages about what you are studying together, encourage them, check in on them, and make sure they know you love them. If you take the time to overcommunicate with them when you have time, it will lessen their need to interrupt you when you don't have the time.

Again, the principle is simple yet somewhat counterintuitive. Spending time to maintain relationships with those you disciple will actually create more time for you so you are ready when unexpected circumstances arise. If you choose to save time by communicating less or cutting corners, you will do so at your own peril. The less you communicate and give attention up front, the more likely you will have problems later. So keep banging that drum!

THE YES OR NO RULE

I have done everything in my power to put boundaries in my schedule so that the impact of interruptions is minimized, but I still find dealing with interruptions to be quite challenging. Interruptions, by definition, cannot be scheduled. Even doing small things like building in extra time in my schedule for lunch just in case something unplanned comes up doesn't always work. That wouldn't have helped with Mike and his moose that night. If we cannot plan for every interruption, what can you and I consciously do with our schedules to help?

I have found a rule that has alleviated much of the stress of planning, something anyone can apply to their own lives. If someone outside my immediate family asks for my time, I listen for the Holy Spirit to give me my answer. Because I have spent time thinking about, preparing for, and looking at my mission and what God has called me to do, I know that the Holy Spirit only says yes when the time spent with another somehow communicates the love of God, makes disciples, brings about repentance, or advances the kingdom of God. If I do not hear a yes from the Holy Spirit, it is possibly because I am trying to advance my own kingdom or increase my popularity with others. In that case, I immediately say no without looking back. When I say no to building my own kingdom, God has more ability to break in and advance his, and I get blessed to be a part of it.

I realize this is easier said than done, and for each of us, the filter of our mission may be different, so here is how you can get started. Develop a mission statement or a set of criteria that must be met before you agree to hand your time to anyone who requests it. For example, my personal mission statement is "I must motivate and inspire people to master the art of relational discipleship." When I am invited to speak at events, jump on video conferences, or receive phone calls asking for coaching advice from other pastors, I ask myself these questions:

1. Is there a possibility that additional disciples of Christ will be made?

2. Will it motivate and inspire others to make disciples?
3. Will there be an opportunity for the art of relational discipleship to be mastered by others?
4. If the answer is no to any of the above, I ask, "Holy Spirit, is this something you want me to do?"

I will admit that following the above guidelines has forced me to say no to many things I really wanted to do. I want to help everyone who reaches out to me. I love serving the Lord and using my gifts in Christian ministry. However, if I were to accept every invitation I receive, invariably one of the people I am personally discipling would need me when I am unavailable. Because I have a set of principles and a clear mission by which I live, I am able to say no to extraneous things and be more interruptible for those I am intentionally helping develop into spiritual maturity. I had a mentor once warn me to be careful about saying yes to the *good* at the expense of the *great*. Being interruptible is only possible when we learn to say no to some things—even good things—but it paves the way for God to act in ways we could never imagine.

THE LENS OF ETERNITY

Continuing on the idea of embracing interruptions, we also need the ability to view our interruptions in a different way. If we know through Scripture that God's plans ultimately prevail, then we must approach and welcome disruptions in our lives as possibly being part of God's design to bring about his will. This doesn't mean every disruption is from God.

Embracing interruptions takes practice. It requires training our desires so we want the same outcomes as God does, even more than I want my own.

Here is a great way to begin this training. Next time an interruption comes, don't look at it as a loss. Instead, get quiet, still your mind, and pay attention to the opportunities God may be presenting to you. First, thank God for the interruption and trust him for the outcome. If we are exercising faith in God, we know that whatever he wills is always what is best. Next, treat the interruption like a treasure hunt—look for the divine nuggets God wants you to find. After all, this day and situation you are facing was "formed" before any of your days came to be (Ps. 139:16). The interruption may be a surprise to you, but it isn't a surprise to God. You can even make a game out of discovering his intentions. This can be wildly entertaining and turn a seemingly unwelcome occasion into a blast. Finally, bask in the glow of allowing God to use you as you see his plan through the lens of eternity. God has a track record for using inconvenient circumstances to bring about his glory. Just ask Moses about the Red Sea and Paul about his thorn in the flesh. Picture yourself surrounded by a "cloud of witnesses" (Heb. 12:1) cheering you on as God is glorified by your reactions to his interruptions.

When I got the call that night many years ago to help a friend, I was frustrated because I wanted to rest and prepare for my speaking engagement at the conference the next morning. I wanted to have a powerful impact on those leaders and do my best to deliver life-changing content. But God had a different story for me to tell, and with it, to minister to a pastor who had never understood what it meant to be intentionally discipled.

And not only that pastor but also many others in attendance as well. Preparation is good, but in that instance God's plans far exceeded anything I ever could have prepared.

What if I had seen the whole moose-packing scenario as a "God opportunity" from the very beginning? I'll never know. But what I do know is that we all must reach the point where we ask God, "What do you have for me?" when we are interrupted as opposed to "Why are you doing this to me?" As I said in the beginning, his plan is always better.

Jesus gave us many examples of how he handled interruptions. Whether it was friends lowering a paralytic through a roof while Jesus was preaching, a woman touching his cloak while he was walking in a crowd, or a centurion asking for healing for his servant while Jesus was traveling down the road, Jesus was able to meet them all in stride and allow his Father to do kingdom work through him. Jesus had time for interruptions.

When the leper in Luke 5 crossed Jesus' path, Jesus didn't let the interruption force him to work longer. As crowds gathered to be healed, Jesus retreated to "desolate" places to pray. He went back to healing after time with the Father. Jesus consistently beat the drum of his kingdom message. Wherever he traveled, Jesus overcommunicated to others what the kingdom of heaven was like using multiple parables and giving ample explanations. Jesus lived a principled life and knew when to say yes and when to say no. Jesus was always about his Father's business and wouldn't let anything stop him from completing it.

Jesus saw interruptions as opportunities to work in tandem with his Father. He always had his heart set in eternity. Whether he was healing, casting out demons, or calming storms, he used the distracting occurrences in his path to strengthen the faith of others and point them toward heaven. We must practice doing the same.

Experience and Apply →

Think back on some interactions with others that you have been involved in recently. Based on those moments, evaluate your ability to be interruptible by answering these questions TRUE or FALSE:

1. During my workday, work takes precedence over other inquiries. _____
2. I don't let another person get a word in during conversation. _____
3. During my free time, it's all about me. _____
4. I don't like to be interrupted during conversation. _____
5. I make time for everyone else and often don't have time for myself. _____
6. When I see someone in need, I stop what I'm doing and assist them. _____
7. People often come to me when they need help. _____
8. Often, I am stretched thin in my normal day-to-day schedule. _____
9. I find time for others when it is asked of me. _____
10. It is easy for me to stop what I'm doing to focus on others. _____

If you answered TRUE to questions 1–4 and FALSE to questions 5–10, let me interrupt you right there—you need to be more interruptible.

Let us explore the life of Jesus during his ministry and see how he dealt with interruptions.

King Jesus' life was filled with interruptions, but he was able to use every interruption to teach and disciple.

READ the stories in Matthew 8:5–13; 9:18–26; and 19:13–15.

ANSWER these questions:

1. How did Jesus respond to these interruptions?
2. What did you learn about the appropriate responses Jesus made in these stories?
3. Think about those who were in close proximity to Jesus. How did their faith change as he made time for them?
4. How can you replicate Jesus' model of being interruptible with those around you?

Jesus is the model we all are to live by. He showed us over and over that being interruptible is a trait that we are to possess to be in intentional relationship with others. By being interruptible, he showed us what it looked like to take time out of his day to teach and disciple those near him. Jesus showed that even with interruptions, he was able to fulfill what he needed to do on a given day by turning the interruptions into opportunities for discipleship.

PRACTICE being interruptible. Every day we have opportunities to capitalize on moments of interruption. Think of the everyday interactions you have and ask yourself if you are interruptible. Are there moments where your agenda is more important than those around you? Put your "yes" on the table. When interrupted, look at the interruption as a time for the Holy Spirit to move others by moving you in that moment. Say yes when asked to give up your time to be in an intentional moment with others.

PRAY that the Holy Spirit will move you to recognize that interruption is okay. Pray for discernment in moments when your agenda may cloud the opportunity to pour into and love someone who may need just a moment of your time. Ask for eyes to see and ears to hear that person, and follow the Holy Spirit in his leading of those moments.

JOSH, A DISCIPLE MAKER

Interruption in my life isn't some blaring story of how I came to the rescue or saved the day. Interruption in my life looks like taking a moment presented to me by the Holy Spirit and addressing his desire for me and that individual who was seeking in the moment.

I have found that as I spend time with the Lord and with those with whom I have surrounded myself, most importantly my family, I have opportunities every day to hear from the Spirit of God during an interruption of "my time." Interruptions often come at random times from members of my family or from my brothers and sisters in faith. Usually they simply need a moment of my time, which I am happy to provide.

This wasn't always the case for me. For most of my forty-three years on this earth, I was a selfish and sin-filled man. You see, my life looked something like this: sleep, wake, work, drink, sleep, wake, work, drink. I found myself in a vicious cycle. I filled my time with everything but God and family—neglecting them because of my selfishness and unwillingness to be interrupted. My son would ask to do something with me, often the smallest of things, but I didn't "have time." My wife would have enjoyed talking with me. She would have been pleased even with something as simple as a hug and kiss before bed or before work, but I was too busy. I did not pause to give my family something they longed for in a father and husband.

One day I found myself in a drunken rage and yelling at my son, just a young boy who was terrified of the man he was casting his eyes upon. I was far from God and didn't want to be interrupted for some petty thing that this child, my son, wanted from me, his father. I was a "believer," but I wanted to rule my own kingdom and not be obedient to the Father in his kingdom. The Spirit of God broke my heart into pieces that day as I laid eyes on my son, who was fearful of the man in front of him, me. From that day forward, my life changed. I viewed myself differently. I recognized who God created me to be, and I vowed to do my part in making important changes in myself in obedience to King Jesus.

As I began to fully trust and rely on the fact that I could not do anything without the leading of the Holy Spirit, I also had to develop relationships with men and women who were obedient in the faith. I found that my ability to be interruptible changed. I began to understand that interruptions are moments the Holy Spirit can and will use to glorify himself through me. Only then could I demonstrate through my actions what it looks like to be loved, no matter the time or circumstance.

The change in me was instantly recognizable to those around me. I became interruptible. My family is ground zero for living this out. I don't do it perfectly by any means, but I have found that the more I give God's time to them, the more they see the change in me, which causes change in them. My son knows that I will stop just about anything to spend a moment with him. My wife knows that if she needs anything from me, I am there for her. Spending time with people who

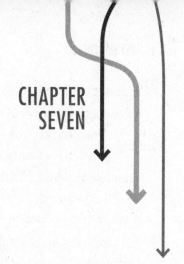

CHAPTER
SEVEN

SPEAK TRUTH

We sat stuck, horns blaring around us as traffic ground to a halt. I wiped sweat from my brow as the diesel fumes began making my eyes burn. We were in the heart of Ethiopia's capital city, Addis Ababa, and caught in horrible traffic. Our worst traffic jams in America pale in comparison to the choking congestion of that city. After many trips here to visit friends and churches, you would think I would be used to it. But I wasn't. I was tired and impatient.

Staring out the window at the throngs of people, cars, motorbikes, and even an occasional donkey pulling a cart, I was stressed. I can't remember what I was worrying about, but apparently my quiet, distant gaze tipped my hand. My dear Ethiopian friend, Desalegn, who was sitting at my side in the van, called me back to reality.

"Brandon, I am so grateful you and the team are here. We are going to have a great day of training!"

I heard his words, mixed with the other conversations going on in our van. His words of encouragement registered

107

but not enough to pull me from my anxious, racing thoughts. Desalegn's next words broke through.

"Brandon, are you okay?"

I turned my head to him, made eye contact, and gave him a canned response, "Yeah, I'm good. Excited about today."

Desalegn wasn't buying my vague reply. So, he asked again. "What are you worrying about?"

My team and I were in Ethiopia to work with a local church plant we helped establish two years prior. Normally when we are doing one of these trainings, I chat with excited energy. And after a decade of facilitating leadership trainings together, this is what Desalegn expected to hear from me. I can't even tell you what was on my mind that day. All I can say is that I needed to hear the truth Desalegn shared with me.

"Can I say something to you, Brandon?" Desalegn asked.

I looked at him and answered, "Of course you can, my friend."

"I am worried about you. Something is different," Desalegn said. "You just don't seem like yourself."

What transpired next was a conversation about a change Desalegn had seen in my life. I was too close to the situation to see it, and I needed a friend to call it out. At that time, so many things were happening in our church. My four kids were at the peak of life's busyness with college, sports, school, and countless activities. I was speaking at more events than normal, and I had allowed the reality of a busy, full life to steal my joy. Stress and worry had crept in, and my focus had shifted. Here I was, twelve thousand miles away from home, in the midst of God's great work in Ethiopia, and I was letting the worries of life ruin that moment.

I confessed to Desalegn that he was right, and I thanked him for making me face the problem head-on. He looked at me and said, "Brandon, do you think the birds are more valuable than you are?" He was referring to Jesus' assurance in Matthew 6 that we should not worry because our heavenly Father will certainly care for us. He cares for the birds, and we are more valuable than the birds. Desalegn challenged me to get my focus off of things I can't control. In the end, he showed me that I was not enjoying life, and he was spot on.

I made a commitment that day to make some changes and to repent of the lack of trust that had crept into my personal walk with Jesus. Desalegn spoke truth into my life and strengthened my walk as a disciple.

TRUTH NOT OPINION

When I describe *speaking truth* as a vital practice of intentional disciple making, I am not talking about giving advice or sharing your opinion. I am talking about speaking truth from the Word of God. My friend Desalegn shared an observation, then backed it up with truth directly from God's Word. In that moment, God used him through the Holy Spirit's leading. He spoke into my life what he saw and stated truth. And the truth stung. The Holy Spirit convicted me in that moment, and I needed to apologize to Desalegn, our team, and most importantly, to God.

When we intentionally disciple someone, God wants to use us as ambassadors who deliver his truth. Not our version of truth or our opinion of truth—but his truth! When we follow

Christ and abide in his Word, the Holy Spirit gives us truth that he desires for us to pour into others.

Our opinions do not have the power to drive spiritual darkness from someone else's life, regardless of how great we may think our advice or opinion might be. We must speak God's truth to those whom he has given us to invest. When we do speak truth into those we disciple, the result is comfort, security, and peace. When Desalegn spoke into my life that day, yes, it was hard, but I experienced comfort knowing he loved me enough to say it. The truth was like a light guiding me back to where God wanted me to be. With truth comes the security of God's guardrails and confidence from knowing we're on the right track. This brings peace to our anxious souls.

Each disciple in whom we invest is a brother or sister in Christ. We become family and walk together on the journey of the Great Commission established by Christ. When we avoid speaking truth to those we disciple, it is more than a detriment. It is dangerous. Even the church can land itself in a perilous place if it dilutes the truth, buying into cultural norms instead of God's standards. Jesus modeled the principle of speaking truth over and over, and he always did so with love. Proverbs 27:6 says that "the wounds from a friend can be trusted, but an enemy multiplies kisses." Even though the truth may hurt, it's better than being seduced by the flattery of the enemy.

WRESTLING WITH THE TENSION

The difficulty in speaking truth when we disciple someone is often not what we say but how we say it. Real tension exists when we speak truth in love. The likelihood of conflict arising when we speak truth is high. Sin nature, broken beliefs (with both the disciple and disciple maker), and lies we believe clash against the truth. And when we deliver truth to someone, we may be met with defensiveness, fear of abandonment, memories of failed relationships, or even arguments.

Unfortunately, conflict isn't the only difficulty that may emerge. Sometimes we speak truth that is affirming and validating to someone only to have insecurity, false humility, or even pride push away the encouraging words and prevent them from sinking in. On many occasions, I have shrugged off a friend's affirming words. At other times, a person I was discipling spoke truth into my life, and I refused to let the truth of God's Word penetrate my soul.

Again, speaking truth is not to be confused with telling people what they want to hear or appeasing them somehow. I am talking about speaking Scripture into people's lives that validates the work of God. God's Word has the power to turn men and women from failure or doubt to confidence in Christ. When we speak truth into someone's life and tensions arise, we must see them, face them, and press into them.

When do we press in? How do we navigate through the land mines buried in relationships when we deliver truth to someone, whether it be to affirm them or to confront their brokenness? The hardest part of speaking truth is wading into the gray areas of a relationship. We quickly find ourselves in confusing places. What I have learned and applied over the years is a principle I call "God's Part, Our Part, Their Part." When speaking truth, we need to have healthy boundaries and appropriate expectations. Conversations are exponentially more helpful and productive when we know our part and can live well in that space.

GOD'S PART

God is truth, and he communicates his truth to us through the Holy Scriptures. Thus, we can know and trust that God the Holy Spirit will never do anything or lead in any way that goes against his own Word. God does not contradict himself. He is not inconsistent. He always acts in accordance with his eternal nature and character—who he is. We also know that he always does his part, providing wisdom and insight into our relationships and conversations. When Desalegn and I were talking, God put Scripture in Desalegn's mind that I needed to hear. God also gave Desalegn wisdom to know what might be wrong with me and how he could challenge me. As Desalegn shared what God had placed on his heart, the Spirit of God convicted me through that truth and brought me to confess and repent before him. God always does his part.

Problems arise when we try to do God's part for him. Sometimes we think we can play the role of the Holy Spirit, and we immediately move the conversation to an unhealthy place. In one instance, I was discipling a young man, and during our meetings I discovered that he had substantial anger issues. I tried to remain curious, asking questions and praying frequently for him, but I saw little change. I became frustrated that God seemed silent on the matter and felt he was not moving fast enough to change my friend. Because of my frustration, I grew impatient and confronted the young man. My desires and my timeline took over. Unsurprisingly, my impatience damaged our friendship. For several months, we did not meet. And although we reconciled eventually, the relationship was never the same.

The Bible is filled with people who tried to do God's part for him. Moses tried to provide water for the people by striking a rock, and Peter volunteered to carry the cup of salvation. Trust me—it never works out well. So let's take a lesson from these mistakes and stay focused on doing our part. Allow God to work, and trust that he's in control. Then remain in a healthy place, and watch as God does his part.

OUR PART

Have you ever heard the saying "Wherever you go, there you are"? When stepping into a discipling relationship, both parties must be "all in." We both must take that vulnerable seat at the table. And while it is unhealthy to try to do God's part, we are healthiest when we do our part well. We do this, as we saw in the preceding section, by being patient and allowing God to do what only God can do and not trying to take over God's role. When speaking truth into someone's life, we keep healthy boundaries for ourselves and make sure we are communicating with love. Here are three keys I have picked up over the years that can help us do our part well.

1. KNOW the Word

Whether you are discipling someone for the first time or have been doing it for years, you have a responsibility to spend time in the Word of God. You must hide God's Word in your heart (Ps. 119:11). The Holy Spirit will take what you have read and learned and deposit it into someone else's heart. But you cannot give to someone something you don't have. To do your part well, be committed to knowing the Word. Spend time reading it and digesting it.

2. LISTEN to the Holy Spirit

The Spirit of God will bring conviction and reveal truth to you. That is God doing his part. But you must be willing to listen. Learn how God speaks to you, and know his voice. This requires prayer and quiet time with God. In the midst of conversations, pay attention to what God is saying to you in your spirit. Don't drown out God's voice with your own agenda. Listen for the Spirit's quiet voice to speak truth to you for someone else's benefit.

3. SPEAK the Truth Out Loud

You can know the Scriptures and listen to the Holy Spirit, but until you actually speak into someone's life, those things are useless to them. Desalegn cared enough to speak up. He could have backed off, afraid he would hurt my feelings. Instead, he encouraged me, made an observation, and used Scripture to back it up. Desalegn did his part well. You, too, must speak truth in love to those you are discipling.

THEIR PART

One of the lasting truths I have sought to remember as I follow Christ's command to make disciples is a quote I once heard:

"You have never changed anyone." Doesn't that ring true? Neither you nor I have the ability to change anyone. Wouldn't life be so much easier if we could, though? Sometimes I can't help but think how much faster things would go if I did the other person's part myself. If I could just take on that hurt or follow that next step, things would be so much better. But that wouldn't help at all. In fact, it would be a hindrance. In the counseling world, this is called *enabling*, and that's the exact opposite of what God wants us to do.

When we live out the principle of speaking truth into someone's life, we will come face-to-face with the reality that we can change no one. We can speak the truth, but they must respond to that truth and allow God to change them. Sometimes, however, we get frustrated, and we want to give a little nudge or a swift kick to someone moving sluggishly along the discipleship path. Don't do it! Listen to the Holy Spirit's conviction, and take a step back. We can only do our part. It's up to them to do their part. The rest is up to God.

LESSEN THE TENSION

Sometimes we do everything right. We remain in a healthy space with boundaries in place, yet the conversation still goes awry. Tensions flare and conflicts arise. So how can we manage the tension in conversations so that we have the best chance at a healthy outcome? In chapter 1, we looked at listening to understand, and this principle must be practiced to help others. But there are some other tools that will enable us to go even further in our listening. These are ways to go above and beyond any defensiveness or negative responses we might encounter when we are trying to speak the truth in love.

Words of Encouragement

Starting on the right foot is critical when speaking truth, especially if you are confronting broken or dysfunctional behavior. In several of his New Testament letters, the apostle Paul delivered words of encouragement *before* passing along a rebuke. Intentional disciple making means that you are . . . intentional. So use encouraging words that are life-giving and true. Avoid patronizing words or flattery just to make people feel better about themselves. Most people know when you are insincere in your words about them. If a person is blunt or direct, encourage him in his forthright speaking. If a person is kind, generous, or friendly, cheer her on.

Don't just leave it there, though. Tell them *why* their forthright personality or generous spirit has blessed you. Attach your words to examples of positive relational impact. This helps disciples connect relationally with you and helps them see that they are valued in the relationship.

Make Eye Contact

For some of us, making eye contact can be difficult. But the alternative is far worse. Staring off into space or looking at your cell phone can completely ruin a conversation and communicate that you really do not care. So even if it is difficult for you, when you are speaking truth to someone, look them in the eyes. They might look away or struggle with what you are saying, but remember that you are the intentional disciple maker. You must set the environment and lead them through the words of truth. Surprisingly, I have found this to be more difficult when speaking words of praise rather than words of confrontation. Most people have a difficult time believing or hearing good about themselves. Make sure you do all you can to look them in the eyes and even ask them what they are hearing you say. The skill of making eye contact and the practice of listening to understand can be combined into a powerful tool that deeply impacts the person you are discipling.

Avoid Accusations

When feelings get hurt, the natural response is often some form of verbal retaliation. Our sin nature wants to protect and defend. When you speak truth, disciples may retaliate and accuse you of some mistake or misstep. Resist playing the accusation game. Do not return their fire. Take a deep breath, hold strong, and remember that your purpose is to invest in, develop, and walk with them. If a strong accusation comes back, take the time to ask questions. Repeat back to them what you are hearing them say. Stay calm.

You must guard against spouting accusations as well. Even if you are frustrated or disappointed, you must start the conversations with encouragement. If you put aside your personal feelings and let the Holy Spirit speak through you, then you know you are speaking truth and not your own opinions. The Holy Spirit will also bring Scriptures to mind that will back up your words. The ones hearing truth from you will know of your love and concern for them, and hurt feelings will then fade into the background.

THE LOVING-KINDNESS OF GOD

Jesus spoke truth everywhere he went. The Gospels are filled with examples of this. Whether it was in John 3 when Jesus told Nicodemus that he must be born again to enter the kingdom of heaven or in Matthew 23 when he called out the hypocrisy of the Pharisees, Jesus never backed down from speaking truth. Even in John 18, as Jesus faced his crucifixion, he answered Pilate's questions and told him that his purpose for coming into the world was to bear witness to the truth. Pilate still questioned the truth, and in condemning Jesus and washing his hands of the outcome, he turned his back on the truth. We know Jesus *is* Truth, and he spoke truth. Sometimes he clothed truth in shades of encouragement and hope. At other times, truth came dressed in the bold colors of confronting sin. No matter how he spoke, Jesus always spoke truth with the intention of bringing people closer to the Father.

Practicing what Jesus modeled for us and becoming unconscious capable in our disciple making shows up when we speak truth. We function as spiritually healthy disciples, growing closer to Christ, and by doing so, we naturally speak what God speaks through us. The Holy Spirit uses us as messengers to deliver truth to those whom we disciple. Without even thinking about it, our natural response will be to speak truth rooted in the loving-kindness of God. As intentional disciple makers, God calls us to go into the world. This call demands that we speak his truth to those who so desperately need to hear it. Our challenge is to deliver truth in a way that demonstrates the love God has for his children. We carry the healing salve of God's Word to share with those we disciple.

Experience and Apply →

Speaking truth to someone you care about can be difficult. We worry about offending, hurting feelings, or in some cases even ending a relationship. The Bible tells us in multiple places that speaking truth, even when difficult, is correct and best for relationships. The problem that often occurs though, is not in what we say but how we say it. Truth spoken with love and in relationship can greatly impact how well difficult truth is heard.

Most people do not like conflict, and some will avoid conflict at all costs. But intentional disciple making will absolutely put us in the position of having to speak truth. One of the most important principles to remember is "God's Part, Our Part, Their Part." Read the statements below and write a G if it is God's part, an O if it is our part, and a T if it is their part.

_____ Convicting someone of their sin

_____ Responding in a godly way to hearing truth spoken

_____ Softening someone's heart to hear truth

_____ Speaking a biblical truth into a person's life

_____ Praying for God to give wisdom in how truth is shared

_____ Applying the biblical truth once it has been heard

When we speak truth, we can do our part only when we remember that God will always do his. Our goal when speaking truth is to help the person we disciple grow closer to God, ourselves, and others. It's about relationship. (In light of this, your answers should be G, T, G, O, O, T.)

Let's take a look at an example of Jesus modeling healthy conflict in Scripture. Jesus said that the Father is always at work. Jesus modeled for his disciples that he was looking to see where the Father was working. The Father's work is restoration of relationship. Thus, Jesus was often in a position to speak hard truth to those the Father was restoring. Let's look at the story of the woman at the well in John 4:1–26. Here we find Jesus in a conversation with a woman who was living in sin. She likely was shunned by her community, for she gathered water in the middle of the day, after other women had already collected water for their families. Jesus confronted her sin but did it in a way that led her to a greater truth and even to salvation.

READ John 4:1–26.

ANSWER these questions:

1. What did Jesus model to his disciples by taking the time to be with the woman at the well?
2. How did Jesus model speaking truth in love to a woman who might be defensive or riddled with shame?
3. Jesus spoke truth to the woman and confronted her sin but pointed to her greatest need, salvation. How can

you point people to greater spiritual needs when speaking truth into someone's life?

4. Speaking truth might include confronting something difficult or praising someone for a job well done. Both happen when discipling someone. For you personally, which is the most difficult to receive from others when they speak truth into your life? Why?

Speaking truth can cover a great deal of relational ground. Sometimes the greatest truth we can speak is a word of encouragement or exhortation. That can be difficult for people to hear based on their past or their view of self. Remember to season every word you deliver with grace, keeping your goal of pointing people to Christ and building a relationship.

PRAY that God will guide you on the path of becoming intentional in your disciple making. Ask him to give you the right words when speaking truth to those you disciple.

THOMAS, A DISCIPLE MAKER

John and I met at church and began spending time together. Through time and proximity, we began to build the foundation of a lasting relationship.

We planned to meet for lunch one day, and everything was going well. Our conversation bounced around from family to work, to sports and other general topics. The food came, and we began to eat. During our meal and conversation, John suddenly paused. I could tell something was wrong, but I didn't know what it was from our conversation. So I leaned across the table and asked, "Hey, man, what's wrong? What's going on?" He looked back at me and quickly snapped, "Nothing. Everything's good," in response. I knew him, though. This wasn't a "nothing" issue, and it was really affecting him. I raised my eyebrows to tell him, "That response isn't going to cut it." He finally spilled the beans. The burden that he was once uncertain he was ever going to share lifted as he unloaded what was on his mind.

He began to share with me about an argument he and his wife had the night before. A little argument had turned into a major one. Each new line of his story turned into a barrage of complaints, explanations, and arguments for his case.

When he finished, I knew in my heart that I had a choice to stay silent, agree with him, or speak truth to him. A debate began inside my mind. If I were to stay silent, he would see that as agreement with everything he was saying. If I agreed with him verbally, I would be taking sides and joining him in something I knew wasn't right, speaking ill of his wife. The third path was the hardest, but I knew it was right: to share what God's Word says about how we husbands are to treat our wives. I felt like the debate lasted for eternity. I knew the right thing to do was to point John back to truth, but I was worried that he would get upset with me and our relationship would be damaged.

The moment of truth arrived. I looked up at John and asked him if I could share something with him. He said, "Of course, anything." I asked, "John, do you know what Ephesians 5 says about how we are to love our wives?" He replied, "No, tell me." I began to talk about how Ephesians 5 tells us to love our wives as Christ loved the church. I watched as my friend began to hang his head in defeat. He knew his attitude didn't line up with what God's Word said, and I didn't have to explain to him further.

I didn't want to leave my friend's head hanging in shame and defeat, so I said, "John, we can work on this. We can plan to start today." He lifted his head, and I saw a glimmer of hope on his face.

During the rest of the meal, we spoke about what it meant for Christ to love the church and ways that he could show those same characteristics to his wife. We prayed together at the end of our time together and then parted ways.

A couple of days later, I got a phone call from John. He was ecstatic. He said, "Dude! I have something exciting to tell you." I said, "Oh yeah? What's up?" He said, "Remember all of

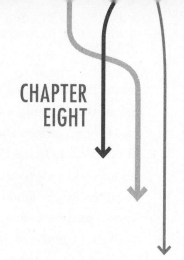

STAND FIRM

My older daughter, Emma, was driving the car the day she and her sister were involved in their life-changing car accident. After five days in the hospital, Emma was released to go home under extreme concussion protocols. Physically she was experiencing lingering headaches, but her pain wasn't just physical. She was also suffering from nagging emotional scars that just would not fade. She could not shake the memories of that fateful day.

Before the accident, both girls had been talented softball players—Olivia the catcher and Emma the pitcher. But the accident had understandably shaken Emma's confidence in her own abilities. Yet despite her nagging worries and fears, she continued to step into the circle and pitch for her high school varsity team. She made it through the first few weeks of the season, but she struggled to throw strikes, and I could tell she was not herself. My wife and I wondered if she would ever be able to return to the level of play she had achieved before.

Then, one Friday night, a home run hit changed everything.

It was the first inning of the game, and the first two batters Emma faced that night had reached base on infield errors. With two runners on base and no outs, the opposing team's best batter stepped up to the plate. My heart pounded. Coaches from a Division I university were in the stands, specifically there to watch Emma pitch, and I was nervous for my girl. After several pitches, Emma threw one right down the middle, and the hitter connected, launching the ball over the center field scoreboard for a three-run homer. My heart dropped. I felt so bad for Emma. I looked over to see if the coaches from the university would get up and leave, but they didn't. They stayed to see how Emma would respond.

I will never forget what she did next. The umpire threw Emma another ball, and she stood outside the pitcher's circle staring in the direction of home plate. She took a deep breath, slapped the ball into her glove, set her jaw, and went to work. I could see resolve on her face, something I hadn't seen before, even before the accident. Emma struck out the next three batters, and on her first at bat, she hit a towering home run to tie the game. Later in the game, she hit another home run and completely shut out the other team with outstanding pitching. Emma's team won that night 9–3, and I watched as this kid, who had been through a car wreck, severe injuries, and the near loss of her sister, stood firm and refused to quit. She displayed a firm resolve to move forward regardless of what stood in her way. That night my daughter taught me a lot about grit and resolve, things we all need in life—and in our disciple making—to move ahead even when everything seems to be falling apart.

So, what happens when we are committed to and living out

intentional disciple making and then life gets hard? Success stories are fun to tell and rewarding to relive, but unfortunately there are also many times when relationships do not end well and people even walk away from following Christ. Walking out the call Jesus gave us is difficult, and he promised it would be. In fact, in Matthew 7:14 Jesus described following him as a narrow path. The gate to the path is small, and few will find it.

Jesus told a parable in which he likened the truth of his Word to scattered seed, some of which took root and grew, but some of which fell on poor soil or was choked out by weeds. He also told stories in which he compared some people to lost sheep or lost coins. As we walk on this journey, we live out those parables by sowing seed and seeking the lost. A commitment to follow Jesus and be an intentional disciple maker comes with not only ecstatic highs but also some soul-wrenching lows.

Several years ago, I was sitting in my backyard with three guys I had been discipling. We prayed for Joe, a man who had become a close friend and member of our group, and our hearts were heavy as we sat in a circle praying for him. At this point, our group had been studying the Bible and doing life together for eighteen months. Joe had now missed our meetings two weeks in a row, and we feared he had left our group for good. Each of us, in our own way, had reached out to him but to no avail. Joe had accepted Christ just before joining our group, but we knew that he had struggled on and off with alcoholism most of his life, so naturally we were concerned for him. Before our group prayer time, I had met with Joe privately because I sensed he wasn't doing well. In our conversation, I challenged him directly and asked if he was drinking again. His anger flared, and he said some hurtful things. I confess I didn't handle his

you. And behold, *I am with you always, to the end of the age"*
(Matt. 28:19–20 ESV, emphasis mine).

Jesus was not giving his people a new promise of being
with them. He was reminding them of a very old one. In
Deuteronomy, God made this same oath to those who love and
walk with him. "Be strong and courageous. Do not be afraid or
terrified because of them [the nations in the promised land], for
the LORD your God goes with you; *he will never leave you nor
forsake you"* (Deut. 31:6, emphasis mine).

When feelings of discouragement, defeat, or loneliness
arise, and the world appears to abandon us, we must turn to
the Lord and not to ourselves. The following three principles—
remembering, resolving, and rallying—will help us stand firm
even when disciple making gets messy.

REMEMBERING

We remember and reflect on the Lord's promise never to leave us.
Years have passed since my girls' car accident, and as painful as
that day was, I still reflect on it from time to time. Often, in a moment of intense struggle, we are blinded by hurt or worry. Time
gives us space to reflect and remember. And as we pause and look
back at those moments, we realize God was right there with us
all the while. In the Old Testament, when the Israelites wanted
to remember something God had done, they would build altars
of stone to remind them of God's work in their lives at that place
and time. We can do that, too, though we don't need to use liter-
al stones. Instead, we forge markers in our minds of God's presence during difficult circumstances and remember his goodness.

When someone who is being discipled breaks off the relationship and leaves the process, our first response is typically to question what we have done wrong. I sometimes become anxious and worry that the person will walk away from the church or from God and never return. Other disciple makers I have talked to wonder if they have let God down in some way. We must remember that we are responsible for doing our part to restore relationship and resolve differences. But we must also understand that the person we are discipling has to do their part as well, and as much as we might want to, we cannot do their part for them.

Although Jesus calls us to participate and we are responsible for our obedience to his call, he is the architect of intentional discipleship. We diminish salvation anytime we remove God's part. The same could be said about taking God's part out of the discipleship process. As we disciple others, he gives us instruction about how to stay healthy in the journey. Jesus calls us to abide in him, to turn to him for the life-giving sap the Vine provides. He modeled this for his disciples. At the pinnacle of his life's difficulty, just before he faced the cross, Jesus sought strength, comfort, and assurance from the Father.

In various ways throughout this book, I have tried to paint the picture that this call to disciple intentionally is murky. The primary color on the palette is gray. We can have the greatest intentions and do our best and still end up with undesired results. This murkiness should lead us to remember who God is and press even further into our relationship with him. There we find what we need that cannot come from ourselves. In Christ we are reminded of who we are to God. We are his children, and he is for us. We reflect on how desperately we need him, for only in him do we find hope. The more we intentionally disciple others, the more desperate for God we become. We will have difficult situations, and this fact should drive us straight to the Father and his Word. Our unconscious-capable response as an intentional disciple maker should always be to remember who God is and what he has done for us, and to stand firm in the mission to which we have been called.

RESOLVING

You must know that you know. Reading the book of Acts always inspires me, especially as I read about the church's responses to persecution. Most of the leaders of the early church spent time with Jesus and had been eyewitnesses to the resurrection. The empowerment of the Holy Spirit gave them resolve. Though they were threatened, beaten, and imprisoned on many occasions, the disciples stood firm in their calling to be fishers of men. Quitting was not an option for most of them. That resolve established a tenacious church that advanced the gospel throughout the Roman Empire.

When we surrender our lives to Christ as Lord, we receive a commission. In the Western church today, we often see this commissioning as optional or required only for those in vocational ministry. Some wrongly believe that disciple making is reserved for those who are extreme—the radicals—or for professionals. But when we read the New Testament and look at the lives of those in the early church, we see that living out the Great Commission was not optional or reserved for an elite few. Jesus' command to go and make disciples of all the nations is to be lived out by all who follow Jesus. Our salvation in Christ connects us directly to his mission. We *all* are called to be intentional disciple makers. We must know that we know. We must resolutely move in the direction of becoming unconscious-capable disciple makers.

When Olivia was going through rehab, we learned that there was no substitution for repetition as she learned to catch a softball again. The countless hours she spent putting on her glove and transferring the ball from her throwing hand to her catcher's mitt each day eventually resulted in Olivia being able to play catch with me again. The action eventually became unconscious capable—she caught the ball without thinking about it. Similarly, our resolve is strengthened by repetition of the process. Familiarity that results from repetition pays off, especially when hard times arise. The first time a person I was discipling walked away, I was devastated. Over time I grew in my resolve. Not only did I become more intentional as I lived a disciple-making lifestyle, but I also had many repetitions under my belt that confirmed that the process of disciple making was the spiritual answer needed by those I discipled. I had seen positive results in the form of changed lives time and time again. Our resolve grows when we see people growing spiritually. We know that we know that true life is found in salvation in Christ and following him in allegiance.

This allegiance should lead us to take inventory of our lives. We must ask ourselves what is more important than living out and accomplishing the Great Commission. Like most parents, I love my kids and will endure tremendous sacrifice to benefit their future. But is providing for my kids supposed to be my highest priority? No! My primary role as their father is to develop my children into committed disciples of Jesus. Resolve to live out the Great Commission requires that I bring all my roles, including husband, father, and friend, into alignment with it.

Living out the Great Commission is sometimes an arduous task. Standing firm when the disciple-making journey becomes difficult or discouraging requires resolving in our hearts and minds that quitting is not an option. Recall how Emma stood out on that softball field, resolved that giving up was not an option. In sports a rough day is inevitable. In disciple making, the question is not *if* someone you're discipling is going to leave, fall, or quit, it's a matter of *when*. Therefore, you must resolve in your heart and mind that no matter what happens you will not back down from the commissioning Jesus gave you.

Our resolve goes hand in hand with the first principle of the practice, remembering who God is. If disciple making becomes difficult and we rely on our own determination, burnout is inevitable, and eventually we will quit. We are not strong enough to accomplish the Great Commission on our own. We must have the power of the Holy Spirit to strengthen our resolve. Together we stand firm. When we remember who God is and his promise not to leave us, and we press into the Holy Spirit as we resolve to keep going, we can then move on to the third principle of the practice—rallying.

RALLYING

We rally others to stand alongside us to link arms as a committed group. My favorite movie is not really a movie; it's a miniseries called *Band of Brothers*. The ten-part miniseries tells the extraordinary story of the men who made up the 101st Airborne's Easy Company during World War II. The story follows these soldiers from basic training all the way until the surrender of Nazi Germany. This group of young men fought together at almost every major event in World War II's European theater, from parachuting into occupied France on D-Day to holding the line at the Battle of the Bulge. They eventually went on to capture Hitler's infamous Eagle's Nest in the Bavarian Alps. Their heroic story always reminds me of the mentality that should exist in the church. Even though this band of brothers lost some of their dear friends along the way, their commitment to each other was what held them together. They rallied as a true band of brothers with common goals. They didn't just want to win the war; they wanted to survive and make it home—together.

Many parallels exist between the physical wars we fight in this world and the spiritual wars fought in the heavenly realms. According to Scripture, we Christians fight in this spiritual war as well. We must do things like train, prepare, and band together as the body of Christ. Jesus not only knew this, but he described it. The apostle Paul used war analogies all throughout his letters to the churches. For us to stand firm on the Rock of our salvation and live out the Great Commission, we must recognize that we cannot do this alone. We must rally together. By nature and by definition, the church is called to be a band of brothers and sisters.

In Luke 13:24, Jesus made a powerful statement regarding being his disciple. "Strive to enter through the narrow door. For many, I tell you, will seek to enter and will not be able" (ESV).

Jesus used the term "strive." The New International Version says, "Make every effort." The term in the Greek is *agonizomai*. We get the English words *agonize* and *agony* from it. In using this language, Jesus was setting up the dichotomy of training versus trying. Jesus was telling us that getting through the narrow gate is difficult, and few will want to do what it takes to enter into the kingdom of God. Becoming a disciple of Jesus Christ means that we die to ourselves and take up our cross and follow him. This is what it takes to walk through the narrow gate. This death to self is not easy. At times it is agonizing. But the freedom we receive from it outweighs any suffering we may face.

So do you see why we need to rally—why we need one another's support to stand firm? We cannot walk this road alone. Much like the men that made up Easy Company in *Band of Brothers*, we must rally together. We hold each other up, locking arms to protect one another from the storms of life, and we do so with wholehearted effort. We train, we strive, and we develop the kind of grit it takes to fight a spiritual war. We help our fellow disciple makers make it to the narrow gate and fight a war where eternity is at stake. We rally together as brothers and sisters in Christ.

THE HARD EDGE

Again, Jesus is our model for intentional disciple making. Nowhere in the Gospels do we find him soft-selling truth to win over someone. Jesus repeatedly modeled a hard edge and clear boundaries that left people wrestling with the truth.

Unfortunately, in the world today, Christians in leadership positions often lean toward setting a soft edge for those they lead, justifying it as love or an effort to win someone to Christ. Jesus did not do this, and he never asked us to do it. Whether it be his interaction with the woman at the well, the woman caught in adultery, or the rich young ruler, Jesus never diluted the truth. Rather, he spoke truth clearly and conveyed it firmly yet in a loving way. He kindly and empathetically called people to repent and follow him. His words were not gentle suggestions but firm calls to obedience and holiness.

So, when we *remember* who Christ is, *resolve* to stay even when life is hard, and *rally* with our fellow Christians, we are better equipped to stand firm. Speaking the truth of the Scriptures to those we disciple becomes who we are, not just what we do, and this is where true disciple makers are found.

Experience and Apply

No calling or mission in this life is more important than the Great Commission. Jesus gave us a mission to go make disciples. This intentional lifestyle comes with incredible highs and sometimes difficult lows. Jesus himself experienced people doubting, quitting, and even rejecting him. When the difficult times come, we must know that we know this mission is more than just an assignment. This calling by King Jesus is a lifestyle that we choose to live that does not give room to walk away, regardless of what others may do.

Throughout this book, I have shared snippets from our

family's life experiences following our girls' car accident. When this tragedy struck, for days we prayed for Olivia to live but prepared for her to pass. I came face-to-face with a reality. I had to ask myself if I would continue to follow Jesus and pastor his people if Olivia went home to the Lord. In those dark moments, I had to decide to stand firm.

Take a moment and reflect on how committed you are to walking out the Great Commission of going and making disciples. Place a check mark next to the statements that apply to you.

_____ Intentional disciple making is brand-new to me. I am not committed until I have more experience.

_____ I am starting to take steps to live a more intentional life. I am unsure of my commitment level.

_____ My life is being changed by intentional disciple making, and I am making a greater commitment each day to stand firm in this calling.

_____ I am sold out! Intentionally making disciples is my life's mission.

Below write a brief explanation of why you chose those statements.

_____

_____

_____

_____

In the book of Acts, we see the apostles facing persecution. They were told to stop preaching about Jesus or face consequences. We see their strong resolution to carry on and be obedient to the mission Jesus gave them before he ascended to heaven. Their conviction was anchored by three factors:

1. They *remembered* what Jesus had promised in word and performed in deed.
2. They *resolved* themselves to the mission, knowing that Jesus absolutely raised from the dead.
3. They *rallied* together to encourage and support each other when times became hard.

READ Acts 4:1–22.

ANSWER these questions:

1. How did the filling of the Holy Spirit impact Peter as he shared that Jesus raised from the dead?
2. How do you see the resolve of Peter and the others with him impact the religious leaders persecuting them?
3. Now read Acts 4:23–31. How did the believers rally together? What impact did that have on the early church in Acts?
4. How can you rally together with other believers to become even more intentional in your disciple making?

In a world where truth is constantly under attack, followers of Jesus might be tempted to compromise or shy away from Jesus' call to make disciples. But when they do stand firm in their commitment, they may be mocked or attacked. Thus, we must know that we know we are called to a lifestyle of intentional disciple making. We must firmly resolve to walk with people and intentionally invest in them. Sadly, some will justify quitting and walk away to choose an easier path. Admittedly the path of disciple making is narrow and filled with challenges. It's the right path, though!

PRAY that God will give you the resolve needed to stand firm in your development as a disciple maker. Ask God to give you relationships with people who will rally with you to start a disciple making movement right where you are.

JUDY, A DISCIPLE MAKER

I am blessed to serve and lead our Restoration Ministry, a team of amazing men and women who have a strong sense of community. We all work hard at staying healthy relationally. We have wonderful, committed volunteers who tirelessly shepherd veterans, unwed moms, people in recovery, and people in struggling marriages. This ministry requires a weekly commitment from most of our volunteer leaders, as well as a good chunk of time discipling people during the week.

On one occasion, a volunteer had a disagreement with a ministry policy, and a conflict arose with some of the other team members. She had served passionately and effectively in the ministry for a few years. This volunteer seeks to be known as a subject matter expert, which is a good thing, unless her need to be right trumps everything else. She also struggles with not being in control and tends to work as many angles as possible to get her way.

I sought out wisdom from an elder and from a friend on staff who were closer to the conflict than I was. We agreed that a face-to-face meeting would be best, and we needed to fight for unity and relationship. As the three of us met over coffee to discuss the challenge, I encouraged the elder and staff member to give me a little background on this current issue as well as their points of view. Together we talked about how to navigate the situation.

Because the issue we were standing firm on mattered, I needed to have a clear understanding of what the volunteer was upset about. We needed to determine what was negotiable and what was nonnegotiable in that area. We needed to ask what things we as disciple makers had to stand firm on and what things we needed to let go of, discuss, possibly pivot on, and/or solve.

We first had to consider the facts. These filters help us determine when to stand firm:

1. Theological issue—nonnegotiable
2. Church culture issue—nonnegotiable
3. Personality issue between leaders—negotiable
4. A preference or long-held traditional way of doing something—negotiable
5. Fighting for relationship—nonnegotiable

In this chaotic and changing world, I have had to rethink what standing firm means to me and how I need to live that out as a disciple maker. I have sometimes had to question my opinions and beliefs and search Scripture. Ultimately I have learned to stand firm and have a deep resolve to work things out with my brothers and sisters in Christ.

The downside of standing firm on the issue at hand was we could lose this high-capacity volunteer leader in a growing ministry that needs volunteers. We would also have to navigate the other volunteer team members' confusion over the departure of this leader and deal with broken relationships, hurt, and misunderstanding. We must always choose to fight for relationships.

Here are the steps we use to stand firm and find biblical resolution:

1. **Ask:** Be clear about why we have asked to meet together. Use a nonthreatening approach, but remain clear that we will be talking about how things are going in the ministry where the person leads or serves.
2. **Model:** Model listening to understand. We take time to listen and make sure we are hearing the whole story. The person sees and hears that we care.
3. **Listen:** Listen for broken belief systems, repeat back their statements, and uncover where they are stuck.
4. **Discuss:** Unpack the challenge together. Try not to be in offense or defense mode. If the issue is nonnegotiable, stand firm on the answer. We want them to hear us when we explain that it is nonnegotiable. But we also explain that fighting for relationship is nonnegotiable, and we want us to figure out a solution together.
5. **Assure:** Tell the person that if they choose to engage in and commit to understanding why we have to stand firm on the issue, there is hope for all of us to continue to do the ministry together. If they continue to argue and go behind the ministry leaders' backs, we will need to talk about taking a break from ministry. We call the break an off-ramp, which has a clearly defined on-ramp back into ministry when they have healed from the situation. Here is where it gets hard, for the ministry could have a setback and participants will wonder what happened,

but we choose to stand firm and not be fearful. We will navigate the fallout in a healthy, God-honoring way.

6. **Schedule next meeting:** Don't ever end a hard meeting without scheduling a follow-up meeting. This should occur before we communicate the outcome to ministry leaders. This allows time to process what was discussed. At the next meeting, they have the opportunity to ask more questions, explain how they feel, and discuss what their next step is.

With the guidance of our eldership, we followed this action plan for dealing with our challenging situation with the volunteer. We ended the meeting by praying for all involved, and we each agreed to do our part in this situation.

I love God's church too much to fail to stand firm on the things that really matter. I also love God's people too much not to handle challenges with grace, mercy, and truth.

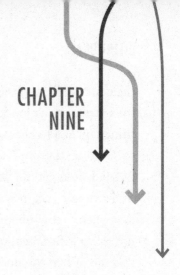

RELEASE
THEM TO GO

"Are you all packed up and ready to go?"

The pediatric neurologist spoke with a smile as she entered the hospital room that had been Olivia's temporary home for two months. Today was the day, and we were realizing the answer to all our hopes and prayers was finally coming true. Our entire family would walk out of the hospital together whole. We spent much of the morning packing up clothes and taking down signs of encouragement people had sent. I remember Amber filling a large manila envelope with all the cards and well wishes that had been sent during Olivia's stay. I remember having an unsettled feeling and wondering if we could provide all the care Olivia needed to finish her rehab and help build back her emotional stability as well. Was she truly ready to go home? Would we be able to make it?

Much of that day we waited for the doctor to come through

the door to tell us it was time to go home. When we arrived at the hospital two months earlier, I would have given you everything I owned to hear those words. All throughout the day, we received texts from friends and family wondering what time Olivia would get out so they could be there to celebrate with us. I struggled again and worried if we were truly ready for this day. Then I remembered the countless hours of rehabilitation, prayer, sacrifice, support, and determination that brought us this far. When the doctor finally came in and asked us if we were ready, Olivia said it best with a huge smile across her face, "Absolutely. I want to go be a kid again."

The hospital doors swung open to reveal Olivia and Emma holding hands. We were greeted with cheers, flowers, balloons, and what felt like our entire church family. It was a day I'll never forget. The celebration in the parking lot of the hospital that day was incredible, and when I reflect on it, I cannot help but compare it to what the Bible says about heaven.

In church, we often talk about angels rejoicing when a person receives Christ. I absolutely believe they do. I also believe there is a celebration when one of God's kids takes up the mission of making disciples—not just leading somebody to Christ but committing to be an intentional disciple maker. Over the years, I have had the opportunity to see dozens of people in whom I personally invested pick up this mantle, and the euphoria I feel when this happens reminds me of that day Olivia left the hospital. She left behind her identity as a car accident victim and took up the identity of being a kid again.

Releasing someone we've discipled to go and make disciples is very similar. When we fulfill the mission of Jesus by making disciples and then release them to go, we are helping them fulfill the purpose God has for their lives. They are leaving behind their identity as fishermen, or whatever they previously dedicated their lives to, and taking up the identity of being fishers of men.

A TRIP TO ITALY

Michael and Diana have become great friends to my wife, Amber, and me. They started out attending our small group, and over time they grew in the Lord in powerful ways. Week after week, I saw them love others in our group, become more involved in our church, and display passion in investing in the lives of others. Amber and I continued to build relationship with them outside of small group. We shared meals together and talked about Scripture, marriage, and parenting children.

During our discussions, Diana asked several times about the work our church was doing overseas. She and Michael had a desire to be part of our work abroad. Over the years, God had been using our church to plant other churches in Italy, and an opportunity to launch a new church came up. Through prayer in my time with the Lord, I felt the Holy Spirit prompt me to invite Michael and Diana to go with us. So one night after small group, Amber and I invited them to join us on our upcoming trip to Italy to train new leaders and help launch a new church plant.

Michael and Diana were all in, and it was time to go. When we arrived in Italy, I watched them minister to our friends and a new group of disciple makers who were raised up there. They helped train and invest in the people. The investment made in Michael and Diana over the previous year and a half bore fruit as they discipled others. It was a beautiful sight. They shared Scripture, told Bible stories, taught biblical principles from within small group and from the stage as well. And this all occurred because they were given the opportunity. More and more, I stepped back and allowed them to lead. Seeing Michael and Diana use their gifts and share what they had learned was a joy. Their growth as disciples of Jesus skyrocketed.

The trip to Italy was remarkably fruitful, and we returned home excited but exhausted from the demanding work such mission trips take. Not long after returning home, Michael and Diana saw that they needed to be leading their own small group. They were now disciples who wanted to disciple others intentionally. So Amber and I did what intentional disciple makers must do: we had them apprentice and lead our own small group for several weeks and then launched them out on their own. We remain close friends with them to this day. They lead their own small group and are making disciples, walking in the life of being fishers of people.

Several critical steps must be in place for a couple like Michael and Diana to be released to go make disciples on their own. Throughout each chapter of this book, we have provided practical principles for intentional disciple makers to implement. But even if we practice every principle, disciple making falls short if we don't release them to go out on their own.

When our daughter Olivia walked out of the hospital, Amber and I had fears. Was she ready to be home? What if she fell or her struggle to swallow properly caused her to choke?

All kinds of terrible scenarios filled my imagination, but we had to trust God and take the steps in order for Olivia to continue to rehabilitate back to a normal life. In similar fashion, intentional disciple making can leave us fearful of letting someone go or even taking the next step in our own lives. When I think of Michael and Diana, I could have let the fear of mistakes or even my own pride derail the opportunity for them to lead and to minister to our church planters in Italy.

In times like these, we all must come to grips with an important fact. The process of disciple making is not ours. It belongs to Jesus, and it is guided by his Holy Spirit. You and I just don't have that much control. If we think we do, we are kidding ourselves. We must understand that the result of all the investment in making disciples must eventually end in the celebratory step of letting them go. They go do the ministry. They lead apart from us and invest in the lives of others. And we let them.

THE PRINCIPLES OF RELEASING THEM TO "GO"

So, what principles must we know to live out the practice of releasing disciples to go? Reflecting over the years of small groups branched and individuals released to go, I see four key principles:

1. Give opportunities to lead.
2. Trust the process.
3. Debrief the mission.
4. Celebrate the wins.

Give Opportunities to Lead

When we follow the life of Christ throughout the Gospels, we see Jesus giving his disciples multiple opportunities to participate in the work of the ministry. In chapter 4, we called these "places to play." Whether feeding a crowd or preaching the gospel, Jesus' disciples were given these places to play. Intentional disciple makers must look around for ways to give those they disciple opportunities to lead. They are able to use their gifts to serve others and share in the ministry.

Allow me to clarify what I mean by *lead*. Organizational leadership in the church is a gift given by the Holy Spirit. Not everyone has been gifted to be a leader in the church at the organizational level. So when I talk about leading in this chapter, I'm primarily referring to leading others through the process of disciple making. All disciples of Jesus should be given the opportunity to lead another through this process—whether it's a neighbor, a friend, a son or daughter, or someone the Lord has brought into your life. As we have previously concluded, every Christ follower is commanded to invest in others and help them spiritually grow. In this way, every believer can, and should, be a leader.

Before ever getting on the airplane with Michael and Diana that day, I thought about the opportunities for them once we arrived in Italy. I knew there would be small groups to lead and leadership principles to teach. From experience, I knew that young leaders would be present in our groups with an abundance of questions. So I prepared Michael and Diana to lead those small groups and others as they invested in our Italian friends. I equipped them with the information they needed to answer questions about basic disciple-making principles.

When we arrived, they felt prepared to step into the opportunities provided.

Excitement filled my heart when I watched Michael and Diana step into these opportunities and lead many of the small groups. They even taught in large group sessions. Even though they were nervous and afraid of making mistakes, I knew they needed the nudge. It was in this moment that they had to trust God and allow him to use them in a way they never had. The fruit that came out of those moments occurred because I stepped back and gave them the opportunity.

As you disciple others, think about the things you regularly do. Could you give that job to someone else? For example, maybe someone in your small group becomes ill or is in the hospital. Could someone else make a meal plan for the whole group to help serve that person? Is it possible for someone from your group to go and visit a person in the hospital and pray with them? What about your apprentice? Could he or she lead the group for a few weeks? I actually enjoy it when something comes up now and I am not able to be at small group. This means my apprentice has to lead on short notice and will have to trust God and step out in faith to lead. Take some time to consider what tasks you could hand off to the person you are intentionally discipling. This will prepare that person for the day you release them to go.

Trust the Process

I love the accounts of Jesus' life when he became frustrated with his disciples and their lack of faith. Every year that I remain committed to being an intentional disciple maker, I appreciate the struggles Jesus demonstrated in the Gospels.

When I reflect on my own journey with Christ, I am grateful for the times he has been patient with me even when I stood paralyzed by fear or wrestled with various issues that stunted my spiritual growth. I'm sure you can relate to my thankfulness that the Holy Spirit is patient with us as he walks us through the process of becoming more like Jesus.

To live intentionally means that we must trust the process. However, the process of intentional disciple making will be riddled with moments when people struggle, fail, doubt, or even simply quit. It is in these moments especially that we must trust the process—trust that God is at work and that the Holy Spirit will help us take the next step. As I mentioned earlier, we certainly must do our part, but trusting the process means that when faith seems low or growth has stopped altogether, progress will eventually occur again.

When my daughter Olivia was going through her rehabilitation and was in the process of becoming unconscious capable in everyday tasks, there were countless times when it felt like she was not making any improvement. Some days even resulted in setbacks rather than progress. Fear and impatience filled my heart and mind. Then one of the therapists would remind me that we all must trust the process. God had saved Olivia for a purpose, and he was at work in her.

Right now Jesus is doing a work in you. If you are engaged in that process of discipling someone else, he is at work in that person as well. Regardless of where either of you is today, I want to encourage you to trust the process. Trust that Jesus sees beyond what you can see and has far greater plans than you could ever imagine for yourself and for those whom you disciple. Your job is to trust him and the work he is doing.

Debrief the Mission

When Jesus' disciples returned after being sent out to preach the gospel, Jesus debriefed with them what happened on their journeys. They shared with him about their victories, and he taught them various things. And after teaching a parable, Jesus explained the deeper meaning of it when his disciples asked. He was preparing them for life after he returned to the Father. He wanted them to understand.

I remember sitting in the airport discussing our trip with Michael and Diana before flying back to the United States. I asked them questions about what they learned and about their favorite part. I wanted to know what God had taught them and where they felt they had grown the most during the trip. We had experienced nine intense days together, God had used all of us to advance his kingdom, and I wanted to process all that God was teaching them while it was still fresh in their minds.

In debriefing with someone, it is helpful to identify truths that can be applied. Along with application, it also helps flush out any misunderstandings or incorrect assessments. If, for example, Michael thought he did a terrible job at leading one of the large group times or felt that he failed miserably during a small group session, I could talk through his doubts with him and prevent any confusion from the lies of the devil. Michael did an excellent job and did not fail in any area, and I was able to confirm this when we talked at the airport. Debriefing is a valuable tool for helping fellow disciples. It lets the person being discipled be heard and understood. An intentional debriefing session can derail the devil's desire to undermine great spiritual moments in people's lives.

Celebrate the Wins

I've heard it said that people will aspire to what you celebrate. Unfortunately, for me celebrating does not come naturally. Once a task is accomplished, no matter how difficult it is, my mind moves on to the next thing. My staff and even my kids have taught me to value celebration. It has been a battle. But I think releasing a disciple to go make disciples might be one of the most important things for us to celebrate this side of heaven.

When someone gives their life to Christ, the church does a great job celebrating this in various ways. But we must not stop there. We must not neglect celebrating the continuing process of disciple making and all the wins along the way. When a disciple of Jesus is released to go make other disciples, we should celebrate that the kingdom of God is expanding and advancing. For every disciple maker we release to go, more people will be reached for the kingdom.

Michael and Diana are leading a group and reaching people whom Amber and I could not. The kingdom of heaven is expanding because Michael and Diana were released to go. They were intentionally invested in, given a place to play, guided through the discipling process, and eventually sent out to go on their own. The process of disciple making is being fulfilled, and that is worth celebrating.

KEEP UP THE GOOD WORK

By celebrating the process coming full circle, we communicate to those around us what is important. Whether you are a mom who is intentionally discipling your kids or a senior pastor who is leading a church, I encourage you to celebrate the process of disciple making. Look for opportunities to lead the way in doing so. This will inspire those around you to live out a disciple-making lifestyle. The apostle Paul celebrated at the end of his letters when he listed all the people who had participated with him in the advancement of the gospel. This is also what God will celebrate when we stand before him and he says to us, "Well done, good and faithful servant."

The practice of releasing people to go and be disciples of Jesus who can make other disciples is the life to which we are called. This is the process Jesus modeled for us coming full circle. Seeing people surrender to Christ, follow Jesus, and grow up spiritually to be disciple makers themselves is worth celebrating. We are helping someone learn to understand the Word of God and how it applies to their lives. This isn't just some process we made up or a self-help program pulled off the internet. This process is empowered and guided by the Holy Spirit and modeled by Christ in his Word. When we participate in the process of intentionally making disciples by raising them up and releasing them to go, we are fulfilling the most important mission ever. We are accomplishing what King Jesus asked us to do. What could we possibly do that is greater than this?

We celebrated that day Olivia walked out of the hospital. She got out of bed, dressed herself, tied her shoes, and walked down the hallway and out the front doors of the rehab center. We are incredibly grateful to God for that. Olivia could get back to being a kid again, and we could reestablish a normal life that didn't involve beeping machines and physical therapy. For our family, that day signified much more than just being released from a hospital. We were released to go continue the work of planting a church and investing in those around us with a new appreciation for God and his kingdom. We were released to go make disciples with a newfound passion far surpassing anything we had ever experienced before.

Experience and Apply →

When we invest in people, especially over the course of several years, releasing them can be very difficult. Depending on what we have been training them for, the risks of allowing them to do the job on their own may be very high. If we are contemplating the release of one of our children to go off to college or the military, or out into the adult world, we may face fear. Likewise, there are risks and fears when we release someone we have discipled to go make disciples on their own.

Spend a few minutes thinking about someone you have discipled. What is holding you back from releasing them to make disciples themselves?

_____

_____

_____

The bottom line is this: we serve a God of multiplication, and _we are his plan_ for making disciples in this world. If we hesitate or refuse to release others to go make disciples, we hinder the multiplication process.

Jesus spent most of his time in ministry with his disciples. They followed him and watched him teach, heal, and minister to people. Jesus modeled ministry for them and how to share the good news. He intentionally invested in these people to further the kingdom of God.

Jesus knew he had to prepare them for when he was no longer with them in the flesh. He did that not only by modeling what he wanted them to do but also by giving them opportunities to participate in the mission themselves. Let's consider a time when Jesus practiced releasing his followers to go and lead the movement.

READ the story in Luke 10:1–24.

ANSWER these questions:

1. How did Jesus prepare the seventy-two as he sent them out to go lead disciple making?
2. In what way was Jesus trusting the process as he sent them to places he knew might reject them?
3. Where do you see Jesus debriefing with those who were sent out?
4. What did Jesus celebrate in this story?

Jesus had been living among his followers and teaching them as he went. Before he sent them on this mission, he gave them specific instructions of what to take with them and how to conduct themselves whether they were accepted or rejected. He instructed them to pray, to show humility, and to faithfully do the work of healing and sharing the gospel. When they returned, Jesus spoke with them about what they encountered. They discussed the joy they had at the healing power of Jesus' name. Jesus reminded them not to take pride in what they had done but to rejoice that their names were written in heaven (Luke 10:20). He celebrated with a joyful prayer to the Father and some meaningful words to his followers.

PRACTICE releasing disciples to do their own ministry. Consider the person you wrote about above.

In the next several weeks, how can you create an opportunity for that person to lead the way in making disciples?

_____

_____

_____

What are your concerns about letting go? Begin to pray now that Jesus will help you trust the process.

_____

_____

_____

What are some questions you could ask as you debrief the experience? Making a debrief plan now will help you follow through when the time comes.

_____

_____

_____

How much time do you normally give to celebration? Plan to spend time encouraging and affirming the things that go well as the person you have discipled begins to lead as a disciple maker.

_____

_____

_____

PRAY that God will show you how to give others places to play. Pray that he will equip you to release those you disciple at the right time and in a healthy way. Pray that God will give you a heart for celebrating the multiplication of his kingdom.

DAVID, A DISCIPLE MAKER

Earlier in my football coaching career, I coached a young man who played tight end for me who had plenty of the "tools" necessary to play the position. Even more than that, he had an excellent work ethic, superb attitude, and a gentle disposition. I didn't know at the time what his future would be, but I was certain he would be successful. He always seemed to dial in on the "coaching" I offered that had nothing to do with football but had everything to do with being a better man.

A few years later, I moved on to become the head football coach at a nearby Christian school, where my wife and I decided to enroll our daughters. One day I was surprised and happy to receive an email from the young man who played tight end for me years before, saying that he had become a coach. He was coaching at a local public school down the road and asked if I would be willing to hire him onto my staff because he wanted to learn from me. I brought him on the next year without hesitation.

In addition to winning football games, our program had a man-building mission. We often said that when one of these young men walked into a room, we wanted everyone in the room to thank God that he was there. My new coach/disciple bought into this goal. I don't recall what his faith level was at the time, but he certainly did a great job of playing the part of a Christian football coach and man builder.

After winning a state championship at that school, we had an opportunity to take over a program at a larger school that had a greater platform for us to carry out our mission. My former player, now assistant coach, came with me, and I promoted him to coordinator. Over the years, we worked more closely together, and I noticed a change in him. He said the things I said, did the things I did, and began to publicly and loudly profess his faith. Even though I never made it clear that I was discipling him, I was. I wanted to hand the program to someone who could keep the mission going after I left. He seemed to understand the relationship better than I did, because he started imitating me without me asking.

The day for me to leave the coaching profession came sooner than I expected when I was called into a different career path. I spent my final season giving this young man more and more responsibility and allowing him to speak to the team as a spiritual leader. I began to take more of a back seat, which was difficult but necessary. He began to take the helm. When I stepped off the field for the last time, the school hired him as the lead coach without a search. They valued what we had started and wanted to keep it going.

As I write this, football season is beginning in Texas. For the first time in forever, I am not a part of it. I sent a message to my former player/assistant coach/disciple wishing him the best for the season and reassuring him that he is equipped for the job and the ministry that goes with it. He responded by saying, "I am beyond grateful for your mentorship and belief in me. You transformed my job into my mission. I show up every day standing on the shoulder of a giant! Any impact I have on future teams is touched by your legacy. Love you."

Our relationship over the last twenty-five years has gone from coach/player to head coach/assistant to disciple maker/ disciple to spiritual peers on the same mission. Because I equipped him over the years, this young man has been *released* to carry on the undertaking that I started. Under a new head coach, there is still a football team in Houston, Texas, committed to developing Christian leaders for the world. Because of this reproducible process of equipping and releasing, God's kingdom advances.

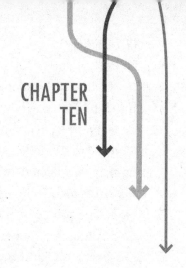

LIVE THE LIFESTYLE

Be faithful with a little is a kingdom principle woven throughout the Scriptures. In Luke 16, Jesus told his disciples the parable of the dishonest manager. Often the parable is taught or preached in the context of giving or managing our material possessions. And while this is a valid application, I believe we need to consider the greater context of what Jesus was saying. He was speaking of the kingdom and teaching his disciples a lifestyle principle. In Luke 16:10, Jesus described this cornerstone principle of a kingdom lifestyle: "One who is faithful in a very little is also faithful in much, and one who is dishonest in a very little is also dishonest in much" (ESV).

This principle tells us that whatever God gives us must be stewarded well, especially in our relationships. Poor stewardship of the things that seem insignificant to us will eventually lead to the destruction of even our closest relationships.

Living the lifestyle of a healthy, intentional disciple maker ultimately rests on how well we steward those little things that make up every relationship. The ability to listen well both to God and to each other calls for good stewardship, as does developing potential and being interruptible. Jesus condemned the Pharisees for the things they put above their relationship with God. The principle of the kingdom is that relationship with God and others should be more important than our material possessions. That's why Jesus responded the way he did when he was asked about the greatest commandment. "Jesus replied: "'Love the Lord your God with all your heart and with all your soul and with all your mind.' This is the first and greatest commandment. And the second is like it: 'Love your neighbor as yourself.' All the Law and the Prophets hang on these two commandments'" (Matt. 22:37–40).

HITTING HOME

Several years ago, I spoke at a conference in the Houston area on disciple making. In my presentation, I focused specifically on how important relationships are to disciple making. I said, "Relationships are the glue that holds the process of disciple making together. Unless we are intentional with our relationships, the process can come apart."

Shortly after I left the stage, I saw a man waiting to talk with me. He introduced himself as Rick, and I learned that he was serving in his church as a senior pastor. He had read several of my books, and I could tell by the look on his face that he had something to say. As Rick thanked me, I saw tears in his eyes. As we stood there together, off to the side of the stage, Rick made a powerful statement that captures much of what it means to live this intentional lifestyle. He said, "Brandon, I have neglected relationships and expected programs to make disciples. I have cared more about making people smarter, not making them more like Jesus." His voice quivered, and I put my hand on his shoulder. He collected himself and finished his thought, "The life of a disciple maker is not about transfer of information; it's about walking relationally with someone while God takes them through spiritual transformation."

"You got it, Rick. You got it," I said.

I remember the validation I felt deep in my soul in that moment. He was listening to what I was saying from the stage. The Holy Spirit was confirming the truth of the Great Commission and the methods Jesus so clearly modeled in the Gospels. Goose bumps spread across my arms. I looked at him and said, "That's one of the truest statements I've ever heard."

When will we fully grasp in the depths of our souls that discipleship is so much more than teaching Bible information? It's more than memorizing verses, parsing the Greek, or expounding doctrines, although those things certainly have their places. When Jesus said to steward the little things in life, the model he gave us was inherently relational. Doctrines give us a foundation of truth to stand on, and memorizing Scripture puts the content of God's Word into our hearts and minds. But they are not ends in themselves. Somewhere along the way, discipleship has moved from a missional relationship where we walk with others, applying the truths of Scripture, to a watered-down program or series of courses intended to transfer information.

Again, disciple making is not primarily what we do—a program or task list of things to accomplish—it's who we are. It's about becoming unconscious capable in every aspect of disciple making. There are practical steps we can take when forging intentional disciple making into a lifestyle, to be sure, but more than tasks to accomplish, these are principles that guide our priorities and shape our lives. Here are some guidelines for stewarding the relationships God has placed in our lives:

1. Do the little things.
2. Prune with willingness.
3. Focus on the fruit.
4. Give permission to rest.

Do the Little Things

I love just about anything that has to do with being outdoors. Much of my life growing up was spent in the foothills of the Rocky Mountains. Whether camping, hunting, or fishing, I spent a great deal of my free time doing something outside. In blogs and in other books I've written, I tell many stories about my adventures in the wilderness.

One thing I love about hiking and hunting is that sometimes I find myself at the bottom of a deep canyon. Maybe I've been out hunting or on a long, adventurous hike, and suddenly I realize that the only way to go is up. In the mountains of northern Idaho, that usually means a steep and difficult climb. Once when I was in high school, my dad and I found ourselves deep in a massive canyon. We faced one of those long, arduous, uphill climbs. With two miles to go and evening approaching,

I wondered if we would get out of the forest and back to our camp in time. I thought we might be sleeping in the woods that night. As we were hiking, my dad said something very true that I remember to this day: "When we put one foot in front of the other and just keep walking one step at a time, we will get out of here." It's amazing how far we can go when we just keep taking little steps, one after another. My dad and I got out of the canyon and back to camp just as the last bit of light disappeared and evening set in.

Jesus talked about doing the little things too. He spoke of the mustard-seed moments in our lives when we practice the art of being faithful with just the little God has given to us. Doing the little things in a discipling relationship means that we take small steps or actions that build others up. Sometimes sending a text or a card, making a phone call, or just giving words of encouragement to the one we disciple can make a large impact. I remember years ago discipling a man named Terry who loved Dr Pepper. He was going through the loss of a loved one, and I brought him a Dr Pepper before we had group one night. That one little thing meant the world to him. He talked about it for months afterward.

In our walks with Jesus, we must learn to do the little things as well. Take time to spend part of your day every day with Jesus. Pause to read Scripture when life is busy or in those moments alone when you just need to quiet your heart and hear from God. Those little things we do matter and help as we walk the journey of life. When we do little things to build relationship with others and also maintain our own relationship with God, we uphold the lifestyle of a disciple of Christ.

Prune with Willingness

As I mentioned in a previous chapter, our team at Real Life Ministries Texas has had opportunities to plant churches in Sicily, a large island off the coast of Italy. I know, I know. You're rolling your eyes and sarcastically thinking how rough it must be to plant churches in such a lovely location. I fully agree that this part of the world is not only beautiful but is home to some of the most amazing people you'll ever meet. Yet as true as that is, it's still not easy. Our partners in Italy face incredible difficulties and persecution. Their commitment to Christ is inspiring, and we've developed amazing friendships.

On one of our trips, we had some free time, and we spent an afternoon walking through a vineyard. It was that time of year when the vinedressers prune back the branches. I love gardening and studying the intricate process of how plant life grows and thrives, and I find it simply amazing to watch how a vinedresser cuts the vine and its branches back so far. If you've never seen it, it looks as though the plant has been killed altogether. And yet that is exactly what is needed for the vines to produce even more fruit than they did before.

We know from Scripture that for spiritual fruit to occur in our lives, the process of pruning must happen as well. Although it is painful, pruning in our lives is astoundingly healthy. For us to maintain lives of intentional disciple making, constant assessment and inspection of fruit must take place, and that also means we must prune. That pruning might be eliminating an activity that is no longer healthy, or it may mean adjusting our diet. It may involve doing an honest assessment of our limits and making a plan to get more rest, or replacing a hobby or habit that no longer serves us well with something better.

Pruning is a discipline. We must be willing to cut and clip and trim things in our lives so that we can bear more fruit. We must also allow God to do some pruning as well. This discipline is necessary to keeping the disciple-making lifestyle productive. So learn to embrace pruning as not only essential but as good. The healthiest vineyards in the world thrive because the vinedresser prunes them every year. Are you willing to be pruned? With the help of God and others, we need to implement this principle into our lives so that even greater fruit can come of them.

Focus on the Fruit

David is our men's pastor at Real Life Ministries Texas, and over the years he and I have become close friends. There are several reasons for this. First, we both are passionate about the mission of Christ and making disciples. Second, we both love sports and the outdoors. Before coming on staff, David was a high school football coach here in Texas, and if you know anything about Texas, you know that football is practically another religion. David was both successful as a coach and highly respected by his peers.

When I first met David, it was not long before I saw a calling on his life to full-time ministry and work in the church. Serving together on the same staff has been a joy, and we have experienced some great conversations. Recently he came into my office, and we were discussing the complexity of disciple making and what "winning" looks like in the church.

"Brandon, sometimes I find it really hard to know whether or not I'm being successful in ministry," David said.

"I feel that way, too, David," I replied. "I think that's why sometimes we gravitate toward counting specific measurables in the church. Sunday attendance, giving, and baptisms are all things pastors want to measure to get a feel for whether or not we are winning."

"Sometimes I work all day here at church and then go home wondering if I accomplished anything. I may have participated in several meetings, met with a church member for lunch, and made phone calls, but I have no idea if I won," David said.

David and I went on to discuss what it means to inspect fruit in the church. What kind of fruit are we looking for that tells us whether we're winning? I explained to him that ministry and football are very similar. Discipling is much like coaching, and we are certainly in a battle with an opposing force. But in football, at the end of a game, we have a scoreboard. The end of the season brings a win-and-loss record that shows if we have been successful. In the church, it's very different. Just because Sunday morning attendance is higher than the national average, that doesn't mean we are winning. Some of the healthiest, most effective disciple makers I've ever known lead churches in small communities or in areas that are hostile to the gospel.

Now, this doesn't mean the fruit of making disciples cannot be translated into numeric measurements. It certainly can. However, the fruit is better measured by the quality of the disciples we're making than the quantity.

The fruit of the Spirit includes love, joy, peace, and patience. Are we partnering with the Holy Spirit to develop those things in people? The fruit we must focus on is seeing people grow in their love for God and others. This is the ultimate trademark of a healthy disciple. Look at the fruit that is considered relational. This fruit comes from the Holy Spirit. It is not necessarily measured in church attendance, the contents of the offering plate, or even the yearly number of baptisms. Those things are good, but the fruit I'm talking about is evidenced by hopeless marriages saved, severed relationships healed, and once bitter hearts now exuding joy.

Give Permission to Rest

The needs are endless. Engaging in a discipling lifestyle means that we get into the mess of people's lives. Discipling practices lead to beautiful things for sure, but the journey can be exhausting. Jesus modeled rest for his disciples. Quiet time alone with the Father was something Jesus did not forsake. So, to stay on the path of disciple making and in the game for life, both physical and spiritual rest must be part of our lives. I have learned over the years that I am in my most unhealthy place when I don't take time to rest. When I'm tired, I find that I have become worn out trying to walk with others and that what I really need is to step back and take a break.

What does that rest look like? For me, it might mean anything from taking the summer off from leading a small group to just taking a day or two to myself and being alone with the Lord. The greater issue for me is giving myself permission to do what is needed to rest and fuel up spiritually. Sometimes intentional disciple makers push themselves too hard and approach burnout. I have experienced this in my own life. So I encourage you to know what is restful for you and to give yourself permission to rest in order to be healthy for the long term. Remember, relational disciple making is a lifelong journey with lots of ups and downs.

I struggled to know when I needed rest, especially in my

first few years of discipling others. My wife played a big part in noticing when I seemed overtired or even became cynical toward the needs of people closest to me. Struggles in others' lives would cause me to withdraw rather than run toward the problem. For every person, the signs or symptoms are different. One of my closest friends, who is a fruitful disciple maker, tends to get irritable or short in his answers with the most basic questions. I know that when he does this, it is time for him to step back and get with Jesus. And in our relationship, I am able to speak that into his life, and he is able to help steer me back to the right path as well. Permission is given when either of us needs rest.

BECOMING UNCONSCIOUS CAPABLE

Four years after the car accident, Olivia accepted a scholarship to play softball at the University of Massachusetts. She truly is a walking miracle and a testimony to the power of God. To this day, she still has a few lingering effects from the accident that cause her to make life adjustments. At times she struggles with her short-term memory, and fading glimpses of balance issues remain. But these are things Amber and I notice because we're her parents. Most others don't perceive these minor deficits. Olivia's journey from learning every physical movement all over again to being a Division One college athlete constantly reminds me of what it takes to be unconscious capable in everyday life. It's hard. It's painful. It takes time. But now my daughter can hit a ball, run bases, and even slap a teammate with a high five—all without a conscious thought.

The most difficult part of the disciple-making journey is making this transition from conscious capable to unconscious capable, and the only way to get there is through intentional effort. Therapists tell us that some movements take more than ten thousand repetitions for them to become unconscious capable. Think about that for a moment. It takes ten thousand repetitions to be able to perform a task or ability in an unconscious-capable way. If we want to become that kind of disciple maker, the kind I believe Jesus wants us to be, we will need to be intentional, repeatedly practicing what Jesus taught us to do.

For some reading this book, the call may seem too challenging. Maybe you are unsure of the path or you don't even know where to start. I want to encourage you to start by taking the first step. Begin this extraordinary journey. There is no end destination until we're home with the Lord. We never truly arrive. Some days you may just work on listening well to someone, and other days you'll notice that you are taking people with you and not even thinking about what you're doing. In some moments, you will really need to concentrate and think about what you're doing. But over time, with practice and intentional focus, the Lord will shape you, train you, and teach you how to disciple like he did. That's what he loves to do.

The journey of intentional disciple making is one of the most beautiful roads you will travel this side of heaven. The call Jesus gave us is not another program or to-do list; it's an invitation to a lifestyle. My prayer is that this book will encourage you to see your life in a new way. Whether you realize it or not, by reading this book, you have taken the first steps on the journey. It won't be long until you look back and are amazed at how far you've come. And never forget, as you regularly live out these practices, it's not what you do that matters; it's who you are. Go and disciple others, teaching them to obey all Jesus commanded. And never forget that he is always with you wherever you go.

Experience and Apply

The most difficult part of the disciple-making journey is when we go from conscious capable to unconscious capable. To become unconscious capable, we must practice thousands of times. This whole intentional disciple-making lifestyle must become who we are, or we simply will never have the repetitions needed to become great at it. Will we ever become perfect? No. Can we honor Jesus by living in such a way that we become the best disciple maker we can? Yes. Take time to reflect on how much you have grown. Put an X by the following statements that have become true about you since reading this book.

1. _____ I am more aware of how to be intentional with discipling another person.

2. _____ I can see areas of my life that are becoming more unconscious capable when it pertains to disciple making.

3. _____ I have become more engaged in the practice of disciple making since reading this book.

4. _____ I could share with someone else some of these practices and help them become a more intentional disciple maker.

How did you do? Did you put an X next to two or more of the statements? I hope you did, and that you are seeing your intentionality grow. Let's explore one final Bible story in which Jesus demonstrated disciple making as a lifestyle.

In Matthew's gospel, Jesus called on his disciples to accompany him to the garden of Gethsemane. In his most difficult time, when it would have been understandable for him to lose focus, Jesus remained close to his disciples and modeled for them what this lifestyle looks like.

READ the story in Matthew 26:36–46.

ANSWER these questions:

1. What was Jesus modeling for his disciples when he called them to join him in the garden?
2. How did Jesus' actions impact the way the disciples went on to live the lifestyle of intentional disciple makers?
3. How can you impact those you disciple by speaking the truth of Scripture into their lives?

PRACTICE being *unconscious capable*. This means that something has fully become a behavior or action we do without thinking about it. It has become who we are. When we do the little things, prune with a willingness, focus on the fruit, and take time to rest, we truly are living out this practice.

PRAY that the Holy Spirit will sink deep within you the practices of being an intentional disciple maker. Ask God to guide and direct you on this journey and to send others to walk with you to obediently accomplish the Great Commission.

ROB, A DISCIPLE MAKER

Everyone who meets me now assumes that I am a people person, but the truth is, for most of my life, no one would have characterized me that way. God may have designed me to be socially outgoing and welcoming, but I railed against his design until I was thirty-two years old. That year I surrendered my life to King Jesus. A few years later, a man I have come to call brother, my good friend, Tim, began to disciple me. Through our relationship, I learned that being a disciple who makes disciples means loving people and meeting them where they are, a fact I have never forgotten. At the point in my life where Tim found me, I did not need someone to speak to me; I needed someone to listen to and understand me. From that gentle start, he taught me to seek God first and assured me that he would be there for me along the way.

Tim's method was simple. Rather than criticize me for my sin and lack of relationship with godly people, he spent time with me, studied the Bible with me, and asked me intentional questions. I did not understand at the time, but Tim was modeling real Christian love through a relational lifestyle. Tim was the first person to truly show me God's love through action. He showed me how to love the person while hating the sin.

Since those early days in my Christian walk, when I meet

people, I do not assume anything. I simply meet them where they are and create a welcoming, relational environment, reflecting God's command, "Love God, love others" (Matt. 22:37–39, paraphrased). One of those people is my friend Benjamin. I met him a couple of years ago and invited him to my small group. He was struggling with brokenness in his current romantic relationship, past hurt, lust, and his identity in Christ. We spent some time together, and I stayed right alongside him, not pushing him to address issues he was not ready to face. After a short time, he quit coming to group and went back to some of his old habits.

About a year ago, Benjamin showed up at small group again, and then we began meeting together one-on-one during the week. We studied a book of the Bible together, and I was able to ask him some thoughtful questions. I invited him to attend the recovery ministry at church with me, but I also invited him to attend my daughter's soccer games with me. As we spent time together, he became more assured of his identity in Christ, he started healing from past hurts, and he even began to volunteer at church. When he started dating Missy recently, he asked me to provide accountability for him because he wanted to approach this new relationship in a healthy, biblical way.

Today Benjamin is walking alongside several other men as they begin to heal from the pain in their past, turn from worldly habits, and learn to live in a way that honors Jesus. Benjamin is living out the reproducible process Christ modeled for us, Tim modeled for me, and I modeled for Benjamin. Being intentional with the people around us impacts the kingdom of God.

ACKNOWLEDGMENTS

I am so grateful that I've had the opportunity to publish several works over the years. This book, in particular, started out in a strange way. At the encouragement of others, I reluctantly tiptoed into this project. Why? In hindsight, I think I was nervous. Scared, maybe? I knew, to the marrow of my bones, this book would be written from who I was. I would tell stories that were personal, like the story of my daughters' horrific car accident. I knew this book was more than just a book to me. It was a look into my own life for others to see. Glory be to God. The Lord used others to prompt, push, and challenge me to pour pieces of my life onto these pages so that others might be inspired to live more intentionally. My hope is that you experience the incredible joy of living out God's holy Great Commission.

Without these individuals this book would never have happened. I want to acknowledge and thank them.

The staff at Real Life Ministries Texas are incredible. Their continuous commitment to Christ and pursuit of disciple making motivated me to write this book. Thank you for your willingness to do the hard things it takes to be a disciple and make disciples.

David Nelson, thank you for being a strong voice and partner in prayer over this project. God used you to help me process content and, more importantly, to say hard things to me that pushed the book forward.

Ron Helle, thank you for being a mentor and a godly man in my life. You exemplify intentionality when it comes to living out the Word of God. Thanks for all you contributed to the book and for being a man of prayer over this project.

Lisa Malstrom, thank you for being a dear friend and partner in all things content driven. Your wisdom, perspective, and desire to see God's kingdom advance makes anything I write possible. Thank you for all your hard work.

Bobby Harrington, thank you for encouraging me to write this book and for all your help to get the project started. I appreciate all of your kind words and recognition that I do my best to live an intentional life. I am grateful for your friendship and partnership in ministry.

NOTES

1. David W. Augsburger, *Caring Enough to Hear and Be Heard* (Huntington, IN: Herald, 1982), 12.
2. Dietrich Bonhoeffer, *Life Together* (New York: Harper & Row, 1954), 25.